ACTING UNDER THE CIRCUMSTANCES

A Smith and Kraus Book
Published by Smith and Kraus, Inc.
PO Box 127, Lyme, NH 03768

First Edition: June 1999
10 9 8 7 6 5 4 3 2 1

Cover and text design by Julia Hill Gignoux, Feedom Hill Design

Library of Congress Cataloging-in-Publication Data
Brestoff, Richard.
Under the circumstances: variations on a theme of Stanislavski: a step-by-step approach to playing a part / Richard Brestoff. —1st ed.
p. cm. — (Career development series)
Includes bibliographical references.
ISBN 1-57525-187-6
1. Acting. 2. Method (Acting) I. Title. II. Series.
PN2061.B73 1999
792'.028—dc21 99-14281
CIP

ACTING UNDER THE CIRCUMSTANCES

Variations on a Theme of Stanislavski

A Step-by-Step Approach to Playing a Part

Richard Brestoff

CAREER DEVELOPMENT SERIES

SK
Smith and Kraus

Dedicated to Mr. Peter Kass, whose inspiration guides me daily, to Ms. Kathleen Park, whose wise advice has been invaluable in the preparation of this book, to Ms. Jenny Stevenson-Brestoff whose patience and help have been remarkable, to Ms. Robin Lynn Smith for her insightful comments, to the many students who helped me to refine this process, and to publishers Marisa Smith and Eric Kraus whose ideas, support, and openness make it possible for writers to write. To all of you, my profound thanks.

CONTENTS

INTRODUCTION

While doing research for my second book, *The Great Acting Teachers and their Methods*, I found myself re-reading the works of that great actor, director and teacher, Constantine Stanislavski. When I got to the end of his last published book in English, *Creating a Role*, I felt stunned. As I read the last chapter entitled, *From Physical Actions To Living Image*, my heart and brain started racing. Stanislavski was making explicit a process of acting that was exciting and different and yet familiar.

As I read, I felt that he was bringing to the surface a way of working that I and others had been unconsciously using for years, but in a vague and undisciplined way. Here on these pages was a clarity that thrilled. I devoured these ideas.

Finally I got to a section of the book called simply, *A Plan of Work*. This consisted of a list of twenty-five points that I presumed were intended as a rehearsal process. And as such it is as brilliant and clear an approach as has ever been conceived.

Stanislavski's list is the outline of what came to be known as the *Method of Physical Actions*. Over the years this has been misunderstood as simply creating emotions through physical movement. But the closer one looks at the method, and the more one hears from Stanislavski's last students, the more one sees that what the method of physical actions asks actors to do, is experience the circumstances of the play emotionally and physically *before* they ever speak the dialogue or try to characterize.

Over the next few months this list and the ideas contained in it kept fighting for my attention. After some time, it began to dawn on me that these ideas had implications beyond the rehearsal process. I wondered why I wasn't sharing this process with my students.

I started to introduce this approach into the acting classes I taught. The results were immediately clear. Here was a way to work in harmony with the actor's instincts. To make the actor want to come out and play. Actors were no longer intimidated by the text but felt instead they could accomplish anything and that it could be fun.

Because Stanislavski's final chapter and list were so short, however, I found that I had to alter and extend some of the ideas. I worked for two years refining this process until I solidified (not petrified I hope) a process that I was able to use and teach. Once this process is understood and experienced in depth, it is remarkably useful for working on material quickly.

With regard to auditions, it should be noted that more and more filmmakers are using improvisation in conjunction with, and sometimes in place of, cold readings to cast actors. The director will set up a circumstance and expect the actor to live believably inside of it. The process detailed here is invaluable in successfully meeting this demand.

Actor training can be divided into two large areas; work on the self, and work on the part.

Acting texts can likewise be divided along these lines. Many contain exercises designed to free the actor's emotions, imagination, voice and/or body. These books tend to focus on sense memory, emotion memory, "substitution," listening and reacting and are aimed at increasing the actor's expressive capacities.

Other acting texts address acting a *role*. Often these books present exercises having to do with objectives, given circumstances, playing character and playing styles. Some books do all of these.

But one looks in desperation for books that detail a clear order of working that builds in a graspable and usable way from one step to the next in a logical sequence. There are such books of course and I would mention here Laurie Hull's *Strasberg's Method*, Uta Hagen's *Respect For Acting,* Moni Yakim's *Creating A Character*, and Robert Cohen's *Acting Power*. But these are the exceptions.

When I realized that these wondrous ideas of Stanislavski's were under-popularized, although certainly not unknown, I thought I would give it a try.

It must be said, however, that I have not been entirely faithful. I have interepreted, added, subtracted, altered, and changed some of Stanislavski's ideas. I did this because in using this process over the last two years I found it necessary to do so. It is remarkable, though, that when I strayed too far, Stanislavski always straightened me out. I have also stayed away from acting jargon for the sake of clarity.

This book follows a pair of actors as they work on a scene from Henrik Ibsen's *A Doll House*. In this way I hope to show this process as it unfolds step-by-step. Some books enumerate exercises unrelated to a text, but such is not the case here. Here, we see how each step builds on the previous one until a coherent process reveals itself.

It should also be noted that this book deals more with work on the role than it does with work on the self, although the actor is constantly being told to work from himself throughout.

The basic premise of this process is that the actor experiences the character's circumstances before she analyzes the text, plays the character, or learns the dialogue. It is a process that allows the actor to organically enter a part and make it his own. It is a way that I think actor's have unconsciously worked for centuries. Some have called it "daydreaming" the part, or "visualizing" the role. Others have called it "intuiting" a part.

It is Stanislavski's great genius that he is able to make such provocative and secret ways of evoking the creative self, accessible to us all.

Richard Brestoff

PART ONE

ACTING DEEP

CHAPTER 1

Letting It Show Business

We're going to see Meryl Streep play Isabella in Shakespeare's *Measure For Measure*. And we're excited. Why? The play itself was a tough read. In fact, long stretches of it cruelly tested our patience. But we're excited because we want to see what Meryl Streep will do with it. We're excited to see if some magical alchemy will occur when this great actress meets this great part. We're even more excited because next week we're going to see Miranda Richardson play the same part. We want to see what sparks will be struck when *this* great actress plays Isabella.

But all of this excitement leads us to a question. Which performance will show us the *true* Isabella? This question leads us on to another; *is* there such a thing as the true Isabella? If there is such a thing, will the two actresses be the same in the part? If they are different and both are terrific, then which is the true Isabella?

Two weeks later we've seen them both and both were indeed brilliant. In fact, while Meryl Streep was playing the role, we could think of it in no other way. But when Miranda Richardson was on stage we could see only *her* Isabella. Afterwards we had our favorite moments for each actress, but while they were acting, we could see the part in no other way. If there is such a thing as Isabella, this should not be possible. And this brings us to a disturbing conclusion: ***There is no such thing as character.***

We remember an amazing moment that Meryl Streep played. A government official who is going to put her brother to death tells Isabella that he will spare her brother's life if she will sleep with him. After delivering this proposition, the actor touched Isabella and left. Just as he disappeared, Isabella/Streep clutched her stomach as her body shuddered with spasms that looked as she was going to be sick right on the stage.

In that moment I understood something that had puzzled me when I read the play. In the play, Isabella goes to her brother and tells him to prepare for death. Apparently she will not do what the government official wants her to do and is willing to let her brother be killed. She will not save him.

Through the centuries, people have tried to understand Isabella's refusal. She is about to become a nun, some have argued, and this would put her immortal soul in danger. Others have said that the proposition is so repugnant that she simply cannot do it. But it was the actress who made it all clear.

It isn't that she *won't* do it. It's that she *can't* do it. Her body refuses to give in even if her mind commands it to. If she goes to bed with the government official her body will freeze, and she will be sick. She will let her brother perish rather than feel that overwhelming nausea and wrenching pain again. *That* I could understand. No intellectual reasons or even moral ones ever quite convinced me that Isabella would let her brother die. But physical revulsion beyond her control? Yes, that I could feel myself.

Isabella only came clear in the playing of her. The actress's response led me to the character. How, I wondered though, did she find such a moment?

What is it that most actors do when they get a part? How do they prepare? First, they read the script through paying special attention to their own part. Then they start concentrating on learning the lines and "finding" the character.

There is a certain panic behind this. What, the actor fears, if I'm no good? What if I can't do this? The danger of this fear is that it can drive the actor into spending precious time and energy on relatively unproductive busy work, like learning lines. At least knowing the words gives the *appearance* of preparation. Everyone at rehearsal will marvel at how quickly you have memorized the dialogue. Unfortunately the lines get learned but the *part* doesn't.

Polonius asks Hamlet, "What's the matter, my Lord?" And Hamlet replies, "Words, words, words." Yes indeed, part of the matter with most actor's preparation is words, words, words. They think acting is talking. And this is understandable. After all, unlike novels or short stories, plays and screenplays are largely composed of dialogue.

In real life, we say our own words, as actors, we say someone else's. This basic difference is what first separates the actor from his part. And the need to make the character's dialogue sound like it's natural to the actor is part of what drives him to learn the lines. But actors must remember that although the lines are the first things they see on the page of a script, they are the last things the author has set down.

What the actor holds in his hand is a final draft; the result of days, weeks, months or even years of work. Before composing the words, the writer constructs a story, creates characters, struggles with the overall structure, sweats the details and rewrites all of these many times over.

The words the actor sees are like the tips of icebergs; they usually conceal more than they reveal. The lines of a script are like a map, and as geographers say, the map is *not* the territory. The thin lines that denote streets on a map in no way resemble the actual potholes, hairpin turns, indecipherable road markings, or washed out edges of the real route. You only discover these at *ground level.*

The other great problem for the actor is jumping feet first into a character. An actor looks at the part of Lenny in Steinbeck's *Of Mice and Men* and decides that the character is slow and retarded. So he puts on his best slow "retarded" voice and walk and that becomes his entire characterization. On the stage or on the screen his portrayal looks like a caricature, and inside he knows something has gone terribly wrong.

Or the actor decides that the character is "mean" or "charming" or "evil" or "heroic" and so dresses heroically, or eats meanly, or walks charmingly. This approach freezes a character into an attitude, which may be fine for a still photograph, but doesn't work in creating living human characters that unfold over time. This need to "characterize" will usually make the actor an outsider to the play and alienate him from a connection between the character and himself. In playing a "character" this way, the actor banishes his own living responses in a misguided attempt to become someone else.

What then is an actor to do? If learning the lines and playing a character are not the best approaches to acting, what is?

The unhappy truth is that most actors have no basic way to prepare. If we go to classes we learn to do character biographies and script analysis. We hear terms like "objective" and "obstacle" and "strategy" used. We try to apply these tools to our acting, and depending on the skill of the teacher and our own native talents we are approximately successful.

But what is missing is a clear step by step *order* of preparation that is consistent with our instincts and feelings. We don't really have a way *in* to the role we are playing that hasn't been intellectually arrived at. So how do we play a character and not lose touch with ourselves? What is a character anyway, and how do you play one?

The simplest, deepest and quickest way for an actor to bring a character to life is to live inside the character's circumstances; to walk a mile in her shoes. But for an actor to do this, he must first walk that character's path *in his **own** shoes.* To lift a character off a page and give life to what is fiction, the actor must lend *her* breath, *her* body, *her* intellect and the beating pulse of *her own inner life* to the character's world.

You, as a living human being, are more fantastic, complex, fascinating and unique than any character ever created. The twists and turns of your mind, the depths and heights of your emotive and imaginative abilities far surpass Hamlet's, Medea's or Willy Loman's. *They* are fictional creations on a page. *You* are alive. If actors *do* become characters, and we are still wondering if that is possible, then the way it happens is through a process of narrowing down, not adding on. The actor must find which sets of personal responses are "right" for the character and which ones do not fit. But if the actor intellectualizes this decision, she will most likely fail to find the full richness of the part.

Our greatest task as actors is to *personalize* the part. The great actor, director and teacher Peter Kass tells the story of working on a Broadway play as an actor. He was playing a character who faces a military execution. At the end of the play he is called into his superior's office and told that all the charges against him have been dropped. His relief is profound.

Kass struggled to find the most true and effective reaction to this news. He tried many choices, falling to his knees, crying, laughing, shaking. None caught what he felt was there. Then one night, by running the circumstance more deeply through his own inner life, he hit on the solution. He had been reacting and then leaving the room. On this night, however, he told an actor playing a guard in the office, to stop him before he went too far. The other actor looked at him, baffled. When Kass was told the news of his pardon, he dully thanked his superior officer, saluted him and started out. Except he wasn't moving toward the office door. He was walking straight out to the audience. Before he fell off the lip of the stage, the guard grabbed him and showed him out.

Kass realized that receiving such good news after steeling himself for death would leave him stunned. No tears, no histrionics. Just a shock so complete that he didn't know where he was. A choice like this can only be found when the actor personalizes the circumstances.

For the actor, intellectual decisions must be based on an emotional experience of the character's circumstances. First comes the feeling life, *then* comes the analysis. And the feeling life that is to be explored is the actor's own.

The great Russian actor, director and teacher Constantine Stanislavski put it this way, "An artist takes the best that is in him and carries it over on the stage. The form will vary, according to the necessities of the play, but the human emotions of the artist will remain alive, and they cannot be replaced by anything else.... You can borrow clothing, a watch, *things* of all sorts, but you cannot take *feelings* away from another person. My feelings are inalienably mine, and yours belong to you in the same way. You can understand a part, sympathize with the person portrayed, and put yourself in his place, so that you will act as he would. That will arouse feelings in the actor that are *analogous* to those required for the part. But those feelings will belong, not to the person created by the author of the play, but to the actor himself."[1]

You cannot borrow the character's feelings. No matter how much you want to, or how hard you try, no matter how much you pay to buy or rent them, you cannot have them for even a little while. The emotions you use to play a character are your own. This brings up the question of emotions themselves.

There are two major areas on which actors must concentrate; work on the *self*, and work on the *role*. Work on the self means being emotionally available. Being emotionally available means being able to feel and to show feelings. This can be hard work. Showing what are private emotions in public can be a daunting challenge. It requires more willingness to *show* than to *hide*, even though the urge to hide is so powerful. It means letting others see more than the comfortable persona we put on every day. It is the true meaning of the business that actors are in: Show Business.

If a strong emotion flushes through an actor he *lets it show*, lets it color his voice, lets it move his body. He doesn't try to

---

[1] Constantine Stanislavski, *An Actor Prepares*, trans. E. R. Hapgood, Routledge *Press*, NYC, 1988, p.176.

squeeze the feeling out or keep it going past its natural life, or banish it altogether. He lets it be. He doesn't manipulate it, he lets it *show*.

Actors are in *Letting It Show Business*. Acting is done in front of people, is a public art, and actors must become comfortable showing the primary colors of emotion and the infinite shades in between. But actors soon realize that if they try to force an emotion to show itself, it will resist; it will likely go off and have a drink by itself at the bar and leave that actor huffing and puffing alone on stage. Emotions need to be lured, not commanded.

It sometimes helps emotions to come out and play when actors realize what makes the acting space different from real life. In your life, the expression of feeling has consequence. If you allow yourself to be thrown into a rage, you may say or do something that has terrible repercussions. You may hurt someone irreparably. But that same rage, expressed in the context of an acted scene, has no effect *outside the world of that scene*. In fact, your scene partner may thank you afterward for giving her so much to play off of. But in real life few will thank you for the hurtful expression of your anger. Understanding this crucial difference can help to make our inner life feel safer about showing itself. But it still is not easy.

Letting ourselves be seen as weak, hurt, tearful, angry, vindictive, sweet or sentimental can make us cringe. Even though the circumstances are *imaginary*, being witnessed by others in ways that are so essentially private, can make us want to hide. This is why one of the prime characteristics of actors is courage. If you are not willing to risk looking like a fool, you will not grow as an actor.

It takes courage to push past the areas in which we are comfortable, it takes courage to go beyond easy charm or reflexive anger; to go beyond the domesticated emotions we allow ourselves to show on a daily basis; to move past our everyday persona's.

Much of acting requires extraordinary bursts of feeling and the control to repeat these on demand. When you enter imaginary circumstances, you must bring your most expressive self with you. In this work, emotions are a sign of strength, not of weakness.

We have said that most actors have no basic approach to a role. Let's now create one. Not a rigid formula to follow slavishly, but a clear and usable template that enables actors to work both deeply and quickly. Let's dive into the business of letting it show.

CHAPTER 2

This Is A Story About...

When the film *Tootsie* was being developed, the writers, producers, and star tried to explain what it was about in a single sentence. This is a crucial but difficult thing to do because that sentence has to capture the essence of the piece without falsifying it. They struggled and struggled to find this sentence. They knew that when they did, that selling and making the movie would only be a detail. If they could boil it down, then everyone would be on the same artistic page, they would all be making the same picture and every scene could be judged essential or not depending on if it served that sentence. It would serve as a compass that would keep them from getting lost.

Finally, they found it. *Tootsie*, they finally realized, is the story of a man who becomes a woman and becomes a better man for it. That's it. Simple and elegant. *How* the man becomes a woman is a detail of the storytelling. In what *way* he becomes a better man for his experience is also a detail. But from this sentence, everyone now had a grasp of the Big Picture. Anything that didn't fit this vision, could be considered a dead-end path.

When an actor reads a play or screenplay in which he is to appear, he should likewise boil it down to a single sentence. Doing this can require great effort. First, the actor must read the material many times.

The first time an actor reads a play is a special time. It is when first impressions are formed, and we all know how powerful first impressions are. The actor needs to shut out distractions like the television, the computer, the phone, other people. All of her concentration must be directed toward the material at hand.

As the actor reads, she should keep a pencil and notebook nearby. When we read, we have many silent conversations in our heads; conversations with the author, the characters and ourselves. These usually go on without our conscious awareness, but they go on nevertheless. If we can capture even some of these impressions they may prove to be invaluable.

As you read, write down any words or phrases that enter your mind; they may seem irrelevant or silly, but write them down. Inventor and designer Buckminster Fuller always carried a notebook with him. He said that if you don't write down an idea within fifteen minutes of having it, you may lose it forever.

When the great director Ingmar Bergman was working on a production of Henrik Ibsen's play *Ghosts*, he kept a notebook of his impressions during his early readings. Close to opening, he still didn't have an over-arching framework for the play.

In some desperation, he went back through his notebook. There he found he had written the word "red." At the time the significance of this word eluded him. He regarded it as some irrelevant and fleeting bit of mental detritus that surfaced for no apparent reason. But now, it's full force struck him.

Red is the color of blood, and a strong theme of the play is how the sins of the father are passed through the blood to the children. He found his framework in that word. He made the walls of the rooms red and carried the color through in startling ways throughout the production. If he hadn't kept a record of his impressions, he never would have found this inspiration.

After reading the play through several times and writing

down any and all impressions that come up, the actor is ready to try some sentences. Some guidelines in doing this are useful.

The actor is looking for a *plot* level sentence. It is not what might be required in an English or a Literature class. This is an *actor's* breakdown of a script.

Now what do we mean by plot level? For help, we can profitably turn to English novelist E.M. Forster's definition of a plot. It is not enough, he says, to say that the King dies, the Queen dies. No, this according to Forster is not a plot.

But if one says, The King dies, the Queen dies *of grief*, then you do have a plot. The difference is causality; something happens and then because of it, something else happens.

Does the sentence from *Tootsie* meet Forster's definition of a plot? Yes it does. The cause of the man becoming a better man lies in his becoming a woman. It implies a change over time. If we keep the *Tootsie* example and Forster's definition in mind, we can try this ourselves.

We have chosen to read Henrik Ibsen's play *A Doll House* in the translation by Rick Davis and Brian Johnston published in 1995 by Smith and Kraus. If you do not know the play, now is a good time to discover it.

To help us boil the play down to its essence, we recount to ourselves its core circumstances.

Early in her marriage, Nora Helmer finds that her husband Torvald has contracted a life threatening disease. The doctors have told her that only a trip to a healthier climate in the south can save him.

Nora keeps this bad news from her husband fearing that the worry will make him worse. But then she is forced to figure out a way to get him to travel. She tells him that he should indulge her wish to go to Italy and even suggests that they take out a loan. This idea however, "really set him off." To save him, she borrows money secretly and illegally to finance the lifesaving trip, and tells her husband that the money has been freely given to her by her father.

In fact, she goes to a shady loan broker named Nils Krogstad for the money. What she does is secret and illegal because in that time and place a woman could not get a loan without her husband's permission.

Krogstad puts certain conditions on the loan. He requires that Nora's father guarantee the loan by signing an agreement. But Nora cannot bring herself to worry her father, who is on his sick bed, about her husband's illness and so forges his name on Krogstad's document.

Nora's husband knows nothing about any of this. Nora fears that he would be humiliated if he knew he owed her anything and furious that she went behind his back to secure the money. In the intervening seven years, their marriage proceeds as Nora makes secret payments to Krogstad to pay back the loan.

All of this happens years before the play itself begins.

The Helmers live very modestly even though Torvald is a lawyer. Part of the reason is that he won't take cases that he considers "ugly." But just before the play begins, Torvald is appointed the manager of the Credit Bank. This means that they will have money for the first time in their marriage, and as the play opens, Nora is extremely happy. Unlike last Christmas, she can now afford to buy gifts for Torvald, her three children and the maids. Money also means that she will be rid of Krogstad and of her secret payments to him. Nora's worries are over.

But this day before Christmas will prove to be a fateful one for her and the entire Helmer household.

Nils Krogstad has a problem. A problem he thinks Nora can solve. It seems that Krogstad, like Torvald Helmer, was a lawyer and that he used his skills to keep a crime he committed, a forgery, from ever coming to trial.

But even though he avoided criminal prosecution, he could not avoid public humiliation and scorn. And ever since the scandal of his forgery came to light, he has been shunned by the town. No one trusts him and so will not hire him for a decent job.

He won his freedom but lost his reputation. In order to live and feed his two children he has been forced into the illegal loan business.

But a year and a half before the opening of the play, Nils Krogstad's luck begins to turn. He gets a low level job at the Credit Bank, and since that time doesn't resort to his former work as a loan broker. It is his first step back to respectability. But a devastating reversal of fortune is in the wind.

Krogstad learns that Nora's husband, Torvald Helmer plans to fire him from his position when he takes over as the new bank manager. This is a disaster for Krogstad and he goes to Nora to ask her to persuade her husband to let Krogstad keep his job. When she refuses, he threatens to expose the loan arrangement to her husband. When she still refuses, he threatens her with more than the revelation of the loan. He has discovered that Nora has committed the very same crime that ruined him. He tells her that he knows about the forgery of her father's signature and threatens to make her crime public.

Shaken to the core by these threats, Nora tries to talk Torvald into letting Krogstad keep his job, but she is unsuccessful.

Worst of all, she believes that her husband will take all the blame for her actions onto himself in order to shield her from humiliation and criminal prosecution. Nora is desperate and contemplates suicide.

When Krogstad receives official notice of his firing, he leaves a letter in the Helmer's locked mailbox revealing all of Nora's misdeeds to Torvald. Nora does everything she can to keep Torvald from reading it. She tries to break into the mail box with her hairpin, but fails. She distracts Torvald from the mail by getting him to help her rehearse a dance he wants her to perform. But she cannot delay the inevitable forever.

At the end of the play Torvald finally opens and reads the letter. Nora thinks that Torvald will never give in to Krogstad's blackmail. She knows and feels that Torvald will protect her, take the consequences on himself and stand up to Krogstad. But she is in for a shocking surprise.

Nora's husband's blames her for ruining *his* life and happiness. He tells her that none of this must come out because if it does he'll look like an accomplice to her crimes; that his standing in the community will be destroyed. He tells her that he'll have to let Krogstad "do whatever he wants with me—-demand anything he wants, order me around, command me however he pleases, and I can't so much as squeak in protest...all for the sake of some frivolous woman."

Nora is dumbfounded. She begins to see that Torvald Helmer is not the man she thought he was. Nora realizes that he has never loved her, "You just thought it was a lot of fun to be in love with me."

Nora realizes that Torvald has treated her like a plaything, and that in doing so she has no real sense of her own value or true self. She resolves to leave her husband and her children in order to teach herself how to be a full human being.

Then Nora Helmer walks away and literally slams the door shut on her marriage.

This simple summary leaves out many details and characters, but recounts the essential elements of the story. Reducing the play to two pages was not an easy task. It could not be done after just one or two readings. It took *ten* readings of the material before this summary was possible. And yet this summary is not set in stone. More readings may encourage us to amend it.

We can always go back and change things.

Aside from extracting a clear idea of the events contained in a play, multiple readings of it serves another purpose. The events and characters work their way into our imaginations without our conscious awareness or effort. They begin to populate an inner landscape within us and take up lodgings there. They start to move and interact, and we silently argue or agree with them, condemn or cheer them, love or hate them. The deeper this teeming well of inner imaginative life becomes, the more the actor has to work with. Let the characters and their situations move in. You will be dipping into this rich pool for creative sustenance for the rest of your journey toward the character.

Now let's carry this boiling down idea further. Let's try to boil the whole play down to a single sentence. What is this play's essence? Part of us wants to say that it's about a woman's struggle for freedom. Or about a woman's need to find herself. But these types of statements, while true, do not fit the Forster or the *Tootsie* examples very well. We try again.

This play is about the consequences of lying. This play is about how society forces people into roles that don't fit them. This play is about the inability of men to see women as full human beings. This play tells us that marriages built on falsehood and deception will crumble.

We're stuck. Because while all of these statements are true, they don't really help us. We are trying to construct themes like we were taught to do in English class, but they don't really serve an *actor's* purpose. We remember some of Stanislavski's advice, "Do not believe the teachers of literature. Put your faith in your feelings."[1]

Let's look again at our examples. The *Tootsie* sentence said that one thing caused another; a man became a woman and became a better man for it. That just feels right. The E.M. Forster example did the same; the King dies, the queen dies of grief. Yes, one thing caused another. There is something else they have in common. They both mention the characters. OK, we ask ourselves, what does Nora do that leads to something else happening?

Maybe that is the way we should construct our sentence. Well, she keeps a pivotal truth from her husband. She never tells him that she has taken out a shady loan and forged her father's signature on a loan document in order to afford the

---

[1] Stanislavski, Constantine, *Creating A Role*, trans. E.R. Hapgood, Routledge Press, NYC, 1989, p. 37.

trip to Italy that saves his life. She wants to keep this truth from him. And does something happen because of this action? Yes, in keeping this truth from her husband, a much more devastating truth comes out; that he is not who she thought he was.

Wait a minute. Have we just backed into a usable sentence? Can we say that this play is the story of a woman who, while attempting to conceal one truth discovers another? Maybe. This does feel a little better. It involves a character and contains some action where one thing leads to another at least. We feel we're getting a bit closer.

Is this a story about a woman who discovers that the man she loves is a stranger? Yes, it's about this too. Can we put these two ideas together? Is this play about a woman whose lies to her husband lead her to discover the truth that he is a stranger? Yes, but we still don't feel that we've penetrated to the play's essence.

Nora doesn't just lie, she sacrifices for her husband. When we think about the play some more, we realize that she pays a price by keeping this loan a secret. She uses the small amount of money that she gets from Torvald not on herself, but to covertly pay back Krogstad. She even takes in work like sewing, embroidering and copying and spends whatever she has on clothes for the children. This loan has cost her. She has even put herself in danger of criminal prosecution.

Is this the story then of a woman who puts herself in jeopardy for the man she loves only to discover that he is a stranger? This feels closer. But we don't think that we've arrived yet. We can say one thing: The struggle to boil the play down to an essential sentence is forcing us look more deeply at the play.

We try some more. We say that *A Doll House* is the story of a woman who, in trying to mask the actions she takes to save her husband's life, winds up unmasking his true nature. This contrasts the idea of "masking" and "unmasking" and has some meaning for us.

In a way, Nora wears many masks throughout the play; the mask of the obedient wife, the mask of the flirt with Dr. Rank;

the mask of the sexual plaything for Torvald. Certainly this sentence tells us about an important aspect of the play. We leave it alone and move on to another sentence.

This time we say that the play is the story of a woman who tries to be everything her husband wants her to be only to discover that *he* is not what she wants *him* to be. Nora does think that he will stand up for her, take all the blame for her misdeeds on himself and he, in fact, *doesn't* do this.

We stop for a moment as a thought flashes across our mind. We wonder if we have ever thought someone to be one way and they turned out to be something else altogether? We ask ourselves if we can think of anyone who has personally let us down in our own lives. And a more disturbing thought comes right behind it. We wonder if we ourselves have ever let anyone down. Several answers come to mind, but we refuse to dwell on them. But the inner pot is cooking.

We try another sentence. *A Doll House* is the story of how a woman's desperate efforts to keep her husband from discovering the truth about her results in her discovering the truth about him. Well, this is true. But it doesn't seem to have enough weight to it.

We seem able to boil down many sentences that are right, true and correct. But we are looking for more than this. We are looking for right, true, correct and *useful*. Useful in that it stimulates our actor's imagination. Dryness is our enemy. We need to get closer to the *feel* of the story, we need its ground level life, we need the story's heart as much as it's head. "Put your faith in your feelings," Stanislavski said.

What then is this story *really* about, at ground level?

Well, a marriage is destroyed and a family is shattered when a woman learns a devastating truth about her husband and her life.

Can we then say that this play is about how the lies a woman uses to hold her life together lead to truths that blow her life apart?

That sentence does involve a contrast between openness and concealment, and that is central to the play. It involves the scope of the consequences that the lies and truths lead to. It has cause and effect; the attempt to hide one truth leads to the uncovering of another. And best of all it *feels* good. We decide to use this sentence as our overall guide.

This then is the story of how the deceptions a woman uses to hold her life together, bring to light truths that split her life apart. This is the foundation we will stand on.

Let's now follow two actors through the next steps and see how and what they create from it.

PROCESS REVIEW

1. **Read the material several times** (ten readings are recommended) with a pencil and notebook. Remove all distractions and read through *from beginning to end in one sitting.* Write down all first impressions no matter how irrelevant they seem.

2. **Distill the whole piece down to a right, true, correct and *useful* sentence.** Try many until you have one you can believe in and work with. Use the *Tootsie* example and E.M. Forster's definition of a plot to guide you.

CHAPTER 3

This Is A Scene About...

The following arrived today:

(She and the children play, laughing and shouting, in the living room and the adjoining room to the right. At last Nora hides under the table; the children come storming in, searching, not finding her; then, hearing her muffled laughter, rush to the table, lift the tablecloth, and discover her. A storm of delight. Meanwhile, there has been a knocking at the front door; no one has noticed it. Now the door half-opens and Krogstad appears. He waits a little while the game continues.)

We recognize this as the beginning of the first scene between Nora and Krogstad from Act 1 of Henrik Ibsen's play, *A Doll House.*

The teacher is playing a bit of a game with us. He is sending scenes to people's homes to work on by themselves. He then will work in class on the process he is trying to teach us. I see I'm playing Krogstad.

At least I know how to begin; read the play through several times and boil it down to its essence. He says that in doing this we are coming very close to Constantine Stanislavski's term, "super-objective." But, says the teacher, he is trying to avoid acting jargon as much as possible.

People, he says with a half smile, argue too much about it. For those of us who like such jargon however, he explains that Stanislavski coined this term to explain the basic purpose of a play, its overriding vision. Our teacher tells us that such a super-objective acts like the North star to an explorer; it helps us to find our way if we get lost. Such a super-objective is like a touchstone against which we can test the other decisions we make as we try to create our role.

We have already boiled the whole play down to a sentence that we like, and realizing that we can change it as we work on the part, we now try the next step. According to our teacher, the next thing to do is to boil the **scene** down to *its* essence.

When we do this for a scene, we are supposed to do something a little different than when we do it for a whole piece.

For a scene, the sentence should be right, true, correct, useful and *playable*. In other words, we should boil the scene down to its core action. We need to find what, at its base, is really going on in the scene. We need to find its pulse.

In order to do this we need to read the scene several times, so we continue:

KROGSTAD: I beg your pardon, Mrs. Helmer.

NORA: (*Turns with a stifled cry, half jumps up.*) Ah! What do you want?

KROGSTAD: Excuse me. The front door was open—somebody must have forgotten to shut it.

NORA: (*Rising.*) My husband's not here, Mr. Krogstad.

KROGSTAD: I know that.

NORA: Well—what do you want?

KROGSTAD: A word with you.

NORA: With—? (*To the children quietly.*) Go in with Anne-Marie. No, the strange man won't hurt mama. When he goes we can play some more. (*She leads the children in to the room on the left and closes the door after them. Now, tense and nervous.*) You want to speak with me?

KROGSTAD: Yes, I do.

NORA: Today—? But it's not the first of the month yet—

KROGSTAD: No, it's Christmas eve. It's up to you how much Christmas cheer you'll have.

NORA: What do you want? Today I can't possibly—

KROGSTAD: We won't talk about that right now. It's something else. I suppose you have a moment?

NORA: Well, yes; all right—though—

KROGSTAD: Good. I was sitting over at Olsen's restaurant and I saw your husband going down the street—

NORA: Oh yes.

KROGSTAD: With a lady.

NORA: So?

KROGSTAD: I wonder if you'll allow me to ask if that lady was Mrs. Linde?

NORA: Yes.

KROGSTAD: Just arrived in town?

NORA: Yes, today.

KROGSTAD: She's a good friend of yours?

NORA: Yes, she is. But I can't see—

KROGSTAD: I also knew her at one time.

NORA: I'm aware of that.

KROGSTAD: Really? That's what I thought. Well then, let me get right to the point: Is Mrs. Linde getting a job at the bank?

NORA: Why do you think you can cross-examine me, Mr. Krogstad? You, who's just one of my husband's employees? But since you ask, you might as well know: yes, Mrs. Linde got a job. And I arranged it all for her, Mr. Krogstad. Now you know.

KROGSTAD: As I thought.

NORA: (*Pacing the floor.*) Oh, I should hope that one always has a little bit of influence. Just because one is a woman, it doesn't follow that—when one is in an inferior position,

Mr. Krogstad, one ought to be very careful with somebody who—

KROGSTAD: Who has influence?

NORA: Exactly.

KROGSTAD: (*Changing tone.*) Mrs. Helmer, would you be good enough to use your influence on my behalf?

NORA: What? What do you mean?

KROGSTAD: Would you be kind enough to make sure that I keep my inferior position at the bank?

NORA: What do you mean? Who's trying to take it away from you?

KROGSTAD: Oh, you don't have to play the innocent with me. I understand perfectly well that your friend doesn't want to run the risk of seeing me again; and now I also understand who to thank for being let go.

NORA: But I promise you—

KROGSTAD: Yes, yes, yes. But here's the point: There's still time, and I'd advise you to use your influence to prevent it.

NORA: But, Mr. Krogstad, I have no influence at all.

KROGSTAD: No? I thought a minute ago you said—

NORA: I didn't mean it that way. What makes you think I've got any sort of influence over my husband in things like that?

KROGSTAD: Oh, I've known your husband since we were students together—and I don't believe our bank manager has any more will power than any other married man.

NORA: You talk like that about my husband and I'll show you the door.

KROGSTAD: The lady has courage.

NORA: I'm not afraid of you any more. Soon after New Year's I'll be done with the whole business.

KROGSTAD: Now listen to me, Mrs. Helmer. If it becomes necessary, I'll fight to the death for my little job at the bank.

NORA: Yes, it looks that way.

KROGSTAD: And not just for the money—that's the least of my concerns. It's something else—well, all right—you know, of course, like everyone else, that some years ago I was guilty of an indiscretion.

NORA: I think I heard something about it.

KROGSTAD: The case never came to trial, but even so every door was closed to me. So I had to go into the sort of business you're familiar with. I had to find something—and I think I can say that I've been far from the worst in that line of work. But now I want to put all of it behind me. My sons are growing up. For their sake I want to win back as much respect as I can in the community. That position in the bank was the first rung in the ladder for me. Now your husband wants to kick me right back off the ladder and back into the mud again.

NORA: But for God's sake, Mr. Krogstad, it's just not in my power to help you.

KROGSTAD: That's because you don't have the will to do it—but I can force you to.

NORA: You wouldn't tell my husband that I owe you money?

KROGSTAD: Hmm—what if I did?

NORA: That would be shameful. (*Choking with tears.*) That secret— my pride and joy—if he learned about it in such a horrible way—learned it from you—. You'd put me through such an unpleasant scene—

KROGSTAD: Only unpleasant?

NORA: (*Vehemently.*) Just try it! It'll only be worse for you. Because then my husband will really get to see what kind of man you are, and you'll have no chance of keeping your job.

KROGSTAD: I asked you if all you were afraid of was this unpleasant scene here at home?

NORA: If my husband finds out about it, of course he'll pay you off immediately, and we'll have nothing more to do with you.

KROGSTAD: (*A step nearer.*) Listen, Mrs. Helmer: either you've got a terrible memory or a very shaky grasp of business. Let me get a few facts straight for you.

NORA: How do you mean?
KROGSTAD: When your husband was sick, you came to me for four thousand, eight hundred kroner.
NORA: I didn't know where else to go.
KROGSTAD: I promised to get it for you—
NORA: And you did.
KROGSTAD: I promised to get it for you on certain conditions. At the time you were so wrapped up in your husband's illness, that I suppose you didn't think through all the details. Maybe I'd better remind you of them. Now: I promised to get you the money based on a note that I drafted.
NORA: Yes, which I signed.
KROGSTAD: Very good. But below your signature I added some lines to the effect that your father would guarantee the loan. Your father was to sign there.
NORA: Was to—? He signed it.
KROGSTAD: I left out the date. Your father was supposed to date his own signature. Do you remember that?
NORA: Yes, I think so—
KROGSTAD: Then I handed the note over to you so you could mail it to your father. Isn't that the case?
NORA: Yes.
KROGSTAD: And of course you did that right away—because only about five, six days later, you brought me the note, with your father's signature. And then you got your money.
NORA: Well? Haven't I been meeting my payments?
KROGSTAD: Yes, more or less. But to return to the question that was a difficult time for you, wasn't it, Mrs. Helmer?
NORA: Yes, it was.
KROGSTAD: Your father was very ill, I believe.
NORA: He was very near the end.
KROGSTAD: He died soon after that?
NORA: Yes.
KROGSTAD: Tell me, Mrs. Helmer, do you by any chance recall the date of your father's death? Which day of the month, I mean?

NORA: Papa died on the twenty-ninth of September.

KROGSTAD: Quite correct; I've already confirmed that. That brings us to an oddity that I simply cannot account for.

NORA: What kind of oddity? I don't understand—

KROGSTAD: Here's the oddity, Mrs. Helmer: your father countersigned the note three days after his death.

NORA: How? I don't understand—

KROGSTAD: Your father died on the twenty-ninth of September. But look at this. Here your father has dated his signature "October 2nd." Isn't that odd, Mrs. Helmer? (*Nora is silent.*) Can you explain it to me? (*Nora remains silent.*) Here's another remarkable thing: the date "October 2nd" and the year are not written in your father's hand, but in a hand I ought to know. Now, that could be explained; your father forgot to date his signature, and someone else did it for him, somewhat carelessly, before anyone knew of his death. Nothing wrong with that. Everything hinges on the signature. And that *is* genuine, isn't it, Mrs. Helmer? It really was your father himself who signed his name there?

NORA: (*After a short silence, throws back her head and looks firmly at him.*) No, it wasn't. *I* signed Papa's name.

KROGSTAD: Listen, Mrs. Helmer—do you understand that this is a dangerous confession?

NORA: Why? You'll get your money soon enough.

KROGSTAD: Can I ask you—why didn't you send the note to your father?

NORA: Impossible. Papa was so sick. If I had asked him for his signature, I'd have had to tell him what the money was for. I just couldn't tell him, in his condition, that my husband was dying. It was just impossible.

KROGSTAD: Then it would have been better for you to give up the trip.

NORA: No, impossible again. That trip was to save my husband's life. I couldn't give that up.

KROGSTAD: But didn't it occur to you that you were committing a fraud against me?

NORA: I couldn't worry about that. I certainly wasn't concerned about you. I could hardly stand you, making up all those cold conditions when you knew perfectly well how much danger my husband was in.

KROGSTAD: Mrs. Helmer, you obviously don't have any idea what you've implicated yourself in. But let me tell you this: what I once did was nothing more, and nothing worse, and it destroyed me.

NORA: You? Are you trying to get me to believe that you risked everything to save your wife?

KROGSTAD: Laws don't care much about motives.

NORA: Then they must be very bad laws.

KROGSTAD: Bad or not, if I produce this paper in court, you'll be judged by those laws.

NORA: I don't believe it. Doesn't a daughter have the right to spare her dying father from worry and anxiety? Shouldn't a wife have the right to save her husband's life? I don't know the law very well, but I'm sure it must say somewhere in there that these things are legal. You must be a very bad lawyer, Mr. Krogstad.

KROGSTAD: Maybe so. But business—this kind of business we're in— don't you think I know something about that? Good. Do what you want. But hear this: if I get thrown a second time, you're coming with me. (*He bows and goes out through the hall door.*)

NORA: (*Stands for a moment, reflecting, then tosses her head.*) Nonsense! He's trying to frighten me! I'm not all that naive. (*Starts gathering up the children's clothes, but soon stops.*) But—? No, impossible. I did it out of love.

So that's it, the scene we are to work on. Just about six pages worth. I read it through several more times and take notes of the thoughts that cross my mind. I sit back and reflect on what I've read.

This woman begins this moment of her life happily playing hide-and-seek with her children and ends it with her whole world in danger. A new thought strikes me. Aren't Nora and Krogstad just playing a very different kind of hide-and-seek in this scene? A much more serious one. And doesn't Krogstad win, successfully flushing out the secret of her forgery?

This scene is a crucial one because it sets the rest of the play in motion. Before this scene, Nora's life is on the upswing. Torvald will soon begin a new job, money will be coming into the household and her payments to Krogstad will end. *After* this scene, however, Nora's life is filled with fear and panic. She must do whatever she can to keep the facts of the loan and her forgery from being revealed.

When I look at my notes I see that I have written the question "why?" several times at different points in the scene. I wrote this because I wondered why she doesn't simply tell her husband the truth? I further wonder why she has *never* told him the truth. She wouldn't be in this situation if she had. Well, maybe I'm getting ahead of myself. I will look at these notes later.

According to our teacher, I must now boil the scene down to a sentence. I don't think I'm quite ready to try this, so I read the scene again. In fact, I read the whole play again.

OK, that's better. I feel ready to try.

This is a scene about a woman standing up for herself, not allowing herself to be bullied.

Well, yes, she does stand up to Krogstad a few times but this doesn't seem to be what the scene is about. It's not the core situation even though it's true. We need a playable circumstance for this sentence. Something that will entice our imagination. Something that will make us *want* to do it. This *wanting* to do, says our teacher, is the lure we use to entice our emotions to show themselves. Maybe we can come up with a sentence that will involve both of the characters and be something that lures our emotions.

The character that keeps moving the action forward in a

scene we are instructed to call the *leading* character. The other character we call the *led* character.[1] In this scene Krogstad definitely pushes the action forward, so we consider him the leading character. When we form our sentence, our teacher wants us to formulate it from the leading character's point of view.

So what does the leading character do? He threatens Nora with exposure. So can we say that this scene is about a man threatening a woman with exposure? At least we have both characters in the sentence, and it's from the leading character's point of view. But it feels too general. What do we mean by exposure? What's really going on here at ground level? That's the level we need to get to, so let's be real. There is a name for what is going on here: Blackmail. Let's call it what it is.

So then is this a scene about a man blackmailing a woman? Yes, it is. But can we usefully say more? *Why* is this man resorting to blackmail? Well, he's being fired by Nora's husband from a job he desperately needs, and he hopes he can get Nora to make her husband give him that job back. That's why he's blackmailing her. So let's try this sentence: This is a scene about a man blackmailing a woman in order to save his job and his status. Is that the core of the circumstance in this scene? Yes, we think it is. At least on a plot level. Do we want to do it? Well, it does seem like wicked fun to blackmail someone. We must admit it does kind of excite us. So we're going to start with this sentence and see where it leads us.

We have now read the play, boiled down a sentence for it, read the scene, and boiled down a *playable* sentence for *it*. What do we do now?

---

[1] These terms appear in an excellent book by Irina and Igor Levin, *Working On the Play and the Role*, Elephant Paperbacks, Chicago, 1992. They use a more strict definition of an "event" there than I do here, and it is well worth looking into.

PROCESS REVIEW

3. **Read the scene you are working on several times** with a pencil and notebook nearby. Turn off the television, radio, CD player and telephone while you work.

4. **Boil down the essence of the scene to an accurate, true, useful and *playable* sentence.** Identify the core circumstance at ground level: What is going on in the scene?

CHAPTER 4

Walking A Mile

In class, the teacher makes our next step clear. We are now going to step into the character's world and experience it from the inside.

One of the reasons we become actors, he tells us, is for this very opportunity. And, he says, it is a privilege. Imagine, we get to experience Hamlet's circumstances, we get to live his life, and we get to walk away. Hamlet doesn't get that chance. In the play, he dies.

Nice words. But frankly, we're skeptical. Nearly every acting teacher we study with and just about every acting book we read asks us to "enter" into the circumstances of the play. The problem is, they never explain to us *how to do it!*

How do we move from reading and thinking about the role, to actually acting it? How do we move from our world to Kogstad's or Nora's without jumping to "character" or the dialogue?

The teacher explains. He tells us that we have boiled the scene down to its core, to a playable circumstance, so that we can *use* that core as the basis for a scene of our own creation.

In other words, we are going to improvise a scene using the following situation: A man blackmails a woman in order to preserve his job and status. No other of the circumstances from the play are needed.

The teacher explains that we are not bound by any of the

events in Ibsen's scene except this core circumstance. We can let the scene go where it goes. If the actress finds herself giving in to the blackmail, she can. Even though Nora doesn't. We can violate the play. The only thing we *must* do is play a scene where a man blackmails a woman in order to save his job. That's all. This surprises us, but certainly seems manageable. We are not writers and that worries us, but playing a simple situation like this does seem possible. Even kind of exciting. There is something naughty and delicious in violating the exact events of the scene, something freeing.

We are told two more things. We are to use our own words, not Ibsen's, and we are to play this improvisation as ourselves. But this immediately brings up a problem.

Which of ourselves are we to be? I wonder. We have so many selves, so many aspects to what we think of as "ourselves." Which of these "selves" are we to use?

In every day life, the teacher says, we have different personas. At work for example, we wear our "work" mask. We do this because it serves a purpose. It wouldn't be appropriate to act the same way at work as at a party, so we put on a mask.

We even have a deeper mask that we call our "normal" self. This is the one that serves as our usual self definition: "I'm a laid back guy, or, I'm the type of person who stays pretty cool and doesn't let much get to me."

But whenever we get up from our chair to walk over to the acting space, we must change this. With each step, we should leave behind our normal persona, like a boat leaving a wake behind it, and enter a different emotional and spiritual space that we might call the Divine Normal.[1] Into this space we bring our expressive self, the self that allows us to be hurt, angry, moved, excited, passionate. The self that lets these feelings show, and allows us to express them in action. The self that will take risks. The "letting it show" self.

---

[1] I am grateful to teacher Jessica Marlowe-Goldstein for passing this term down from teacher Jack Clay.

This all gets our heart racing. It's both exciting and nerve wracking. But when we get up to work, will we be "Divine Normal?"

And what about using our own words anyway? Why not use Ibsen's? Our teacher quotes to us some words of the great theater and film director Arthur Penn. He says, "What I mean by inhabiting a role is where is the *actors'* (italics mine) life and emotions in that procedure? When do they begin to figure in it? And I think they should figure sooner rather than later; that the language should be moved back to an appropriate relationship and that the actor's emotions...and physical experiences should begin to surround that role and only when that's happened should the language come up."[2]

The language, or the words of the dialogue, should come *after* the actor has experienced the circumstances from the inside. Then the words will not sound like lines but like spontaneous and connected expressions.

Using your own words keeps you from trying to imitate some character about which you have preconceived notions and helps tell you what *you* think and feel at each moment. What **YOU** feel and think. Remember, that once you've test the play through your own personal experiences, it no longer seems alien.[3]

We check to see if we truly understand what the teacher is saying: Our first experience of the character's situation will be in our own shoes, as ourselves, using our own language. We are not bound by any other of the scene's circumstances or by the author's dialogue.

In a way, we feel as if we are breaking into the characters' house, finding they are not home, and going through their things. We feel like we are spying on the characters' world. If that idea intrigues you, increases your desire to come up here and throw

---

2. From an interview with Arthur Penn on Bravo cable channel's *Inside the Actor's Studio*.

3. Stanislavski, Constantine, *Creating A Role*, trans. E.R. Hapgood, Routledge Press, NYC, 1989, p. 41.

yourself into the circumstance, our teacher says, then by all means, spy. It could be fun.

Diane, my scene partner, and I get together to construct some framework for the circumstance. After a few weak attempts, we come up with an idea.

Diane, we decide, is an important executive at a major software company. The company *I* work for is on the verge of bankruptcy. I have applied for a high paying job at *her* firm but have been turned down. Since we were once lovers, I request a meeting with her hoping she will overturn the rejection and hire me.

We agree that the piece of blackmail I have on her is that the college diploma on her wall is a fake. I know that she never finished college and that she paid to have false transcripts made. We feel this is a good basic structure and decide to try it out.

Before we start, we remind ourselves of what we are doing. We are acting as ourselves inside circumstances we created based on a core situation created by Ibsen.

We are not to be "Krogstad" or "Nora," and we are not to use their words. We are free of the other circumstances of the scene. We do not even have to conform to Ibsen's story. If Diane tries to seduce me in the scene, she can. If I decide to bribe her with money, I can. It's wide open. We know the basic idea and from there we don't know what's going to happen. *Kind of like the characters in a play.*

Diane begins by sitting at a desk reading over some printed out email memos (created by her fertile imagination, of course). I stand outside her door (created by my imagination) about to go in. I ask myself, if it were me about to do this, what would I feel, how would I act? But the very thought pulls me out of the moment.

When I walked over to the "door" from my chair, did I enter the Divine Normal? Well, before I started thinking about what I should feel, I kind of was. At least I was different, I didn't feel casual. My stomach had butterflies. And it wasn't just from the nerves of acting, it was because I felt nervous about doing this to Diane; blackmailing her. A big part of me didn't want to do it. I need the job, but I hate having to do such a terrible thing. I decide to let that conflict live inside of me and work from it, not interrogate it.

I try to collect myself just before I knock on her door. Maybe I won't have to resort to blackmail, maybe she'll be delighted to hire me into her company. This makes me feel better and I knock with the hope that all will go well.

DIANE: Come in. *(He enters. She puts down her papers.)* Steven, hi. Come on in, sit down.

STEVEN: Hi Diane, thanks. *(Sits.)* Nice office.

DIANE: Yeah, can you believe it? Who'd of thought? Want some coffee?

STEVEN: Oh, I always knew you'd be successful, no thanks, with all this corporate stuff.

DIANE: Really? Why?

STEVEN: Drive. You've always had drive.

DIANE: Well, yeah.

STEVEN: And you drove right through the Golden Gate it seems to me.

DIANE: It's a great place to work that's for sure. I get this office, TWO secretaries, or executive assistants I should say, a great paycheck, stock in the company and really good medical benefits. Sometimes I can't believe my luck.

STEVEN: Your luck's definitely been good.

DIANE: Yep.

STEVEN: I'm afraid mine's been a little spotty.

DIANE: Well, I know about your company going under.

STEVEN: Yeah, that's kind of been bad. I mean I need the money, they haven't met the payroll for three weeks, I've got a mortgage and bills and stuff, you know.

DIANE: I know.

STEVEN: And so, I mean I don't know if you know this, but I applied for a position here...

DIANE: I heard.

STEVEN: Yeah, and I was turned down. But Diane, I'm overqualified for the job and I'm a perfect fit for this company.
DIANE: Well, that was a Personnel decision...
STEVEN: Personnel decision? What does that mean? If you put in a word for me all that would change in a second.
DIANE: Steven, I think you think I have more power here than I actually have.
STEVEN: Oh, come on.
DIANE: I'm serious. I can't go around hiring and firing anyone I please. There are procedures.
STEVEN: Diane, please. Look, if you put in a word for me maybe they would reconsider. I'm sure recommendations are part of the *procedure* aren't they?
DIANE: Steven, this isn't fair. Someone applied who just fit the job description a little bit better than you did, and she got hired. That's all. I can't change it now.
STEVEN. So that's it? You won't help me?
DIANE: It's not that I won't, it's that I can't. This was a team decision.
STEVEN: Jesus. You're acting like you don't even know me.
DIANE: Steven...
STEVEN: I'm sorry. Do you think this is easy for me? I know I'm asking a lot, but doesn't our history count for something? Is it all just so cut and dried? Is it all just *business?*
DIANE: No, of course not. Look...oh, I feel terrible.
STEVEN: You know what? This is making me sick. I don't want to be here making you feel terrible. And I don't want to be begging and pressuring you, it makes my stomach turn.
DIANE: Steven...
STEVEN: I'm just gonna go. I'm sorry, I didn't mean to...
DIANE: It's OK.
STEVEN: No, I'm just going to go. I'm sorry. *(Steven goes.)*

Amazing. I just couldn't blackmail her. That was the core circumstance, and I couldn't do it. I feel like a failure, but the teacher is ecstatic. He says that we played truthfully, seemed immersed in the situation and that we played as ourselves. We didn't push for any emotions that we didn't feel, and we didn't try to be playwrights, and this, he says, is good. We took a real step into Krogstad and Nora's world not by talking about it, but by experiencing it directly. And how did it feel? he wants to know.

Both of us explain that it was a world full of anxiety. I felt horrible begging for a favor and Diane felt terrible being thrown into such an awkward position. The teacher wants to know more about the specific feelings that came up. I had, I tell him, feelings of betrayal when she wouldn't help me, and feelings of guilt, shame and embarrassment for even having to ask. Diane felt nervous and suspicious before I came in because she had a good idea what I was coming to see her about. Interestingly, she too felt betrayed that I would use our old relationship to get something for myself. She also felt angry that I put her in this uncomfortable position.

The teacher wants to know if we let these feelings show as strongly as we felt them. We confess that sometimes we did and sometimes we didn't. Did the feelings make you want to do anything? he asks. We're not sure what he means.

Emotions, he says, always make you want to **do** something. For example, when anxiety builds up inside you, your body wants to move. You cannot sit still. You pace, or do the dishes or clean the house. Emotion forces action.

Diane says that her suspicion and nervousness at the beginning of the scene made her put on a mask of friendliness and babble on about her good luck. It even made her go over to the coffeemaker, pour herself a cup of coffee, and offer some to me. Yes, the teacher says, that's what he means.

I tell him that I experienced myself as such a low life toward the end, felt so disgusted with myself, that I had to get up and go. Yes, the teacher says, the *feeling* led to an *action*.

There is that word. *Action*. I have always wondered what this referred to in acting classes before, but never could get a solid grasp on it. Now it's beginning to come clear. Stanislavski, our teacher says, put it this way, "Action is the movement from the soul to the body...from the thing an actor feels to its physical form."[4] The best way to understand this, of course, is to experience it, and we both just did.

The teacher asks us another question. How, he wants to know, did the circumstances we created differ from the one's in the actual scene, and how were they similar to it? Well, the most obvious difference, we say, lies in the fact that there was no blackmail attempt in our scene. True, he says.

Then the teacher wants to know what *other* circumstances were different. This question forces us back into the text. Yes, he says, you have to **read the scene again**, don't you? So many circumstances are different that we hardly know where to begin.

The teacher helps. He asks about the relationship in our scene. We had a history, we tell him. Yes, he says, but so do Krogstad and Nora. But ours was based on love and theirs was based on a business transaction. Correct, he says, and asks for more differences.

Diane says that in our scene I came to her for a job but that in Ibsen's scene Krogstad comes to Nora for her *influence* on Helmer. I say that while this is true, she still had to go to a third party, the "team," for a final decision. I also was asking for her influence and in that way it was similar to Ibsen's circumstances. Yes, the teacher says you asked her to put in a good word for you. Doesn't Krogstad do the same thing with Nora? We agree that he does. He asks for more differences.

We just stare at him. We're stuck. He suggests reading the scene again. We do, and then it hits me. In Ibsen's scene, Krogstad suspects and then believes that Nora conspires with Christine Linde to push him out of his job. He says, "...and now I also understand who to thank for being let go." That circumstance just didn't exist in our scene. Right, the teacher says. But it didn't have to either, he reminds us.

---

4. Stanislavski, Constantine, *Creating A Role*, trans, E.R. Hapgood, Routledge Press, NYC, 1989, p.49.

Your improvisation isn't a test to see how much of Ibsen's circumstances you remember, he says. It's for living inside the core circumstance of the scene *as yourselves*. But it can unconsciously reveal to you what stuck and what didn't.

When we read a play or a scene we really have no idea how much of what we've read has made an impact. By entering it though, we can find out from ourselves what parts of it had real meaning for us and which parts didn't. The parts that don't lodge inside of us will not show up in our improvisation, we'll skip them.

Now the teacher asks us how we were different from, or similar to, the characters. Diane says that she was friendlier than Nora is in the Ibsen scene and that she felt bad not being able to help me. Nora, she says, has no sympathy for Krogstad. Yes, the teacher agrees, you even invited him to sit down, does Nora do that? No, Diane says, Nora in fact doesn't welcome him at all.

What does she do at the beginning of the scene? the teacher asks. Nora, Diane replies, asks Krogstad what he wants twice and only reluctantly let's him in.

Why? the teacher wants to know. Well, there's no pretense of friendliness between them. She doesn't like him at all, says Diane. How do you know that? the teacher asks. After all, he helped her with money when she desperately needed it. Maybe she is grateful to him?

No, she isn't, replies Diane a little defensively. But how do you *know*? the teacher presses. Diane can't quite remember. She admits that maybe Nora should be grateful to Krogstad for helping her. I can't stay out of this.

No, I say. Diane you're right. Later in the scene Nora says why she doesn't like him. It's all the conditions he put on the loan. Nora says, "I could hardly stand you, making up all those cold conditions when you knew perfectly well how much danger my husband was in."

But that loan was a long time ago the teacher points out. Maybe over the years she has gotten to like him more. Now

Diane picks up the ball. No, she insists, there is no indication that she has changed at all towards him.

Imagine, says Diane, Nora has been paying this guy off for the last eight years! And she's had to do it in secret. They must have some meeting place where Helmer would never see them or anybody else who might tell Helmer that they have seen her with Krogstad.

She's had to scrape and save her money and secretly give it to this cold-hearted man so that Helmer will not find out what she did. Each rendezvous would feel like a punishment. No, concludes Diane, I can't see that Nora thinks of him as anything other than an obligation and a possible threat.

The teacher suggests something interesting. He says that we could improvise a scene that is not in the actual play but that is implied. He says we could improvise the scene where Nora goes to Krogstad for the loan. Diane and I look at each other with a twinkle in our eyes. But the teacher says that's enough analysis for now.

Analysis? Truthfully, I didn't even realize that what we were doing *was* analysis. That's such a dry word and what we were doing just now was so alive and engaging.

But the teacher wants us to pick up the improvisation from where we were and to add in the circumstance this time that I actually blackmail her. So we pick up from before I left her office.

STEVEN: Doesn't our past history mean anything? Is this all just business?

DIANE: Oh, come on that's not fair.

STEVEN: We were in love once.

DIANE: Steven...

STEVEN: Well, doesn't that count for something?

DIANE: Look, this just isn't about any of that. And frankly, I'm getting a little pissed off. I can't believe you would come in here and pull something like this. The answer is no, I can't help you.

STEVEN: Great.

DIANE: I mean I hate to be so hard about it but we've already hired somebody else.

STEVEN: Well, I hate to be hard about stuff too, but if you're going to be cold when I need help then I'll just have to be cold back.

DIANE: I don't know what *that* means.

STEVEN: It means I know things about you that you wouldn't want people to find out about.

DIANE: Are you threatening me?

STEVEN: I'm appealing to your self-interest.

DIANE: *What* are you talking about?

STEVEN: *(Getting up.)* Well, maybe there was something wrong with *your* application when you applied for a job at this company. Way back when you were just a human being like the rest of us.

DIANE: Like what?

STEVEN *(At a wall.)* Like this diploma which you so proudly display. See, I know you Diane. I know you were seven credits short when you left college. And I'm willing to bet that this diploma is a fake. Bought and paid for. Look at this thing. *(He runs his finger across it.)* Clean as a whistle. You actually *dust* it. And I'm further willing to bet that if this company finds out it's a fake, you'd be out on your ear. All your perks and benefits out the window. Not to mention your reputation.

DIANE: Why would you do that to me?

STEVEN: I might not. Depends on you. *You* decide what happens to you, not me.

DIANE: This job is the best thing that ever happened to me, Steven. Don't wreck it. Please.

STEVEN: Nothing has to be wrecked, Diane. Not me, not you.

DIANE: Look, even if they do find out, it's only seven credits. After all I've done for this place they'll probably either overlook it or ask me to finish my degree and hide it all under the rug.

STEVEN: If it was just a matter of that, then you'd probably be right. But what *will* get their attention, I think, is the fraud. Is the lying. The deception. How will they ever be able to trust you? You see, the trust will be broken. And they have to be able to trust you don't they? They can't be wondering if you're going around faking stuff.

DIANE: Steven, please. Look, if I explain it to them they'll understand.

STEVEN: Will they? You willing to risk it?

DIANE: *(Pause.)* I'll do what I can to revive your application.

STEVEN: Good. Yes, you bring it back to life. Make a miracle.

DIANE: I hate you for this.

STEVEN: That's too bad because I actually feel a little better. You're doing the right thing, Diane. See you at work. *(He leaves.)*

I did it. I blackmailed her. The teacher immediately wants to know what it felt like. I confess that after I got going it felt great. Did you expect to feel that way? the teacher asks. Not at all, I reply. I never thought that doing something so awful could feel so good. But it was fun. Doing it was completely different than thinking about it. The teacher is smiling. Good, he says. What about Diane? She says she felt angry, then humiliated, then desperate, then numb. Quite a journey in such a short period of time.

The instructor asks if any feelings led to us to any actions. I explain that when I imagined her diploma on the wall that I felt some amalgam of amusement and disdain that led me to run my fingers over it. Yes, the teacher says, that moment was terrific. Your feelings of scorn led to the action of touching the diploma and contemptuously running your fingers over it. Yeah, Diane agrees, that freaked me out. Made me really think you would do what you threatened.

If we are open to them, the teacher explains, our feelings will express themselves in such actions and bring a life and uniqueness to a part that others might overlook.

The teacher tells us that we've taken our first walk in the

character's circumstances. And we've taken that walk in our *own* shoes.

Now it's time to ask two central questions of our experience. How did our circumstances differ or parallel the ones in the scene, and how were we different from or similar to the characters in the scene?

Time for *analysis*, I thought. Good. Last time it was fun. These two questions always drive me back into the text. So I take a moment and reread the scene. Diane does the same. We both note some differences in the circumstances.

For one thing, Diane's secret in our scene was something that Diane did for her own advancement. It had a selfish motivation. What Nora does, she does for Helmer. And for another thing, the consequence of the blackmail would be that Diane would lose her high paying, prestigious and powerful job. For Nora the stakes are more personal. If Krogstad reveals *her* secret, she runs the risk of losing her relationship with her husband.

But as we talk, we realize something else that has so far eluded us. There are *two* elements to Krogstad's blackmailing of Nora. First, he threatens to reveal the loan to Helmer. But when that doesn't work, he goes further. He threatens to expose her illegal forgery. This means that Nora is threatened on a personal *and* on a legal level. And also on a social level. What will people say? What about the scandal? We never thought about so many levels of threat in our improvisation. It makes us marvel at Ibsen's ingenuity.

Now the teacher wants us to look at how we differed from, or were similar to, the characters. Right away Diane says that she gives in to the blackmail in her scene and that Nora doesn't in hers. Diane felt that she couldn't win she says, that there was nothing she could do.

But Nora, she explains, tells Krogstad that he must be wrong about whether the law will take her good motives into account and even if she does feels defeated, she doesn't show it to him.

So is Nora, asks the teacher, better or braver than you? When Diane starts to answer, he cuts her off saying he just wants her to *think* about it.

For now the teacher stays focused on the question at hand and asks her if there are any more differences between her in the improvisation, and Nora in Ibsen's scene.

Yes, she says. I was nicer to Steven when he came in than Nora is to Krogstad when *he* comes in. I mean even if I was a little apprehensive about him being there, I put on the pleasantries, you know, offered him coffee. Nora isn't that way at all with Krogstad. Nora doesn't even seem to want him there.

You said that before, says the teacher. But why not? She doesn't like him because of the conditions of the loan, answers Diane. But the teacher is not satisfied. He says there is more to it than that, and asks us to look at the circumstances of this visit more closely.

Why, the teacher asks, is Nora so nervous? Diane is silent and so am I. We feel like errant school children.

Let me put it this way, says our teacher, where is Nora's husband, Helmer? We start thumbing through the play looking for the answer to this. After a few moments Diane speaks up: Helmer went out with Dr. Rank and Christine Linde.

For how long? the teacher asks. We don't know that, answers Diane. Does Nora know? wonders the teacher. No, replies Diane. And then she picks up the hint. So Helmer might walk in at any moment and find Nora and Krogstad talking together! That would be a *disaster* for Nora because then she'd have to explain to Helmer what she was doing talking to this man! So what does she feel the minute she hears his voice? asks the teacher.

Danger, answers Diane, and panic. Nora doesn't want to be seen talking with him. It might bring to light the whole loan business. *That's* why she's so nervous, says Diane triumphantly. And what actions, asks our teacher, might this feeling lead to? Maybe, answers Diane, keeping Krogstad in the doorway and not allowing him into the room, and then actually getting him *away* from the doorway so that he won't be seen. Nora might also look out the doorway to see if Helmer is coming, it might lead to all sorts of actions. The teacher seems pleased.

How about you Steven, how were you different from, or similar to, Krogstad?

Well, at first of course, I couldn't even blackmail her, but Krogstad seems to have no problem doing it. The teacher stops me. How do you know, he asks, that Krogstad has no problem blackmailing Nora? I have no answer to this.

Just because he actually does it, says the teacher, doesn't mean it's *easy* for him. The teacher asks, do you think he's a coldhearted bastard because he *does* do it? I start to answer but he cuts me off just as did to Diane. He says he only wants me to think about that.

The teacher presses me for more differences and similarities. I didn't drag the whole thing out the way Krogstad did in his scene, I say. In one section, Krogstad leads Nora along with a bunch of questions before he gets to the forgery business, I didn't do anything like that.

Breaking the scene down into "sections" already? asks the teacher. Well, I reply, when I started to get to the blackmail in our scene I definitely felt like a new and different event was taking place. Good, the teacher says, you are naturally dividing the scene into events based on your *experience* of them. Good, good.

By the way, asks the teacher, did you notice who brings up telling Helmer about the loan? Yes, I say, it's actually Nora. She says, "You wouldn't tell my husband that I owe you money?" Right, says the teacher, it's Nora. Krogstad doesn't come in and say to Nora look, if you don't help me, I'll tell your husband about the money arrangement between us, does he? No, we agree, he doesn't.

In fact, asks the teacher, how does Krogstad come in? I take a quick look at the text. He's actually apologetic and respectful when he comes in, I say. He begs her pardon and says "excuse me" to her. She, I comment, is the rude one at the beginning of the scene. So, the teacher asks, when you played the improvisation with Diane, did you come in to blackmail her?

I have to think about this. I mean we said the scene was about blackmail, but in truth I wasn't really there to blackmail her when I came in. I tell the teacher that I really came in to ask Diane a favor. I hoped she would help me land the job at her company and I was only going to use the blackmail if I was forced to. But I didn't really want to go through with it if I didn't have to.

Is it possible, asks the teacher, that Krogstad feels as you did? That he really comes to ask Nora a favor and only plans to use the blackmail if he must? Yes, I reply, it's more than possible. But his circumstance is more complex than mine. He has just been told he will be fired from his job, a job that means more than just material support to him.

Krogstad was a lawyer, like Helmer, at one time, I continue. But when he uses his lawyerly skills to keep his own criminal forgery from ever coming to trial, the whole town finds out about it and shuns him. He is so despised for what he does that no one will ever again hire him as a lawyer. He can't get work anywhere, in fact. To live, he has to go into this loan-shark type of business.

Finally, a year and a half before the beginning of the events of this play, he secures a low level job at a bank and can quit the loan business. This job is his first step back to respectability. He has two kids and their future depends on their father's success. So to be fired from this job is simply devastating to him. He comes to Nora to see if she will help him get that very crucial job back. Krogstad says it this way:

KROGSTAD: Now listen to me, Mrs. Helmer. If it becomes necessary I'll fight to the death for my little job at the bank.

NORA: Yes, it looks that way.

KROGSTAD: And not just for the money—that's the least of my concerns. It's something else—well, all right—you know, of course, like everyone else, that some years ago I was guilty of an indiscretion.

NORA: I think I heard something about it.

KROGSTAD: The case never came to trial, but even so every door was closed to me. So I had to go into the sort of business you're familiar with. I had to find something—and I think I can say that I've been far from the worst in that line of work. But now I want to put all of it behind me. My sons are growing up. For their sake I want to win back as much respect as I can in the community. That position in the bank was the first rung in the ladder for me. Now your husband wants to kick me right back off the ladder and into the mud again.

When I go over the dialogue, so many impressions come over me. Krogstad is so painfully aware of how public his humiliation has been. Those words, "—you know of course, *like everyone else...*" really tug at my heart. He is a kind of public goat. His pride has been so thoroughly shattered, that I'm actually starting to feel for this guy.

The teacher is staring at me. And then a smile comes over his face. Maybe you are a real actor, he says. Maybe, and here he pauses for dramatic effect, there is even a Krogstad.

WORKING AT HOME

By yourself you can practice training your mind to distill the core circumstance from a piece of material by doing it with books you read, movies you see, television shows and scenes you watch, even articles you read. After you see a movie, try to sum up its core story in one sentence. See if your sentence extracts the essence of what you've seen, without it being a generalized thematic statement. Try to stay at plot level. Use the *Tootsie* example and the Forster definition as your guides.

After you have done this with both the play and the scene you are working on, you can move on to the next step.

Use the core sentence you have extracted from your scene and create an improvisation with the same basic circumstance. When you have created your scenario, set up a simple place where the improvised scene will take place. If the scene is in an office, for instance, place yourself behind a desk or table and do what you would be doing *before* the other character enters; *as if this were you in this situation.*

Imagine that the other character comes in. How does that make you feel? Speak from your feeling and do what you feel you would do. If you think you would pop up to shake their hand because their presence makes you nervous, then do that.

When you are working by yourself you are exploring your own responses to the circumstance you are in. Don't be concerned that your scene partner might do something completely different than you imagine them doing. All you are concerned about in an exercise like this is yourself; how you feel in this situation.

You may find yourself experimenting with just the first few moments over and over again in many different ways. Eventually you can make your way through the basic circumstance you are exploring.

After you have done this improvised scene with an imaginary partner, ask yourself two crucial questions. How did my circumstance parallel or diverge from the written scene's? and how was I different from, or similar to, the author's character? In order to answer these questions fully, you will need to read the scene again.

This work on a part at home can also be done completely in the imagination. Some people are able to sit and "see" the working out of a parallel circumstance in their mind. This is fine, although I recommend putting your experience in your body whenever possible.

PROCESS REVIEW

5. **Create an improvisation based on the core circumstance.** Take that playable sentence, which should be the core circumstance of the scene, and create an improvisation based on it. The improvisation can, but need not, follow the other detailed circumstances of the scene. Play the circumstance *as yourself*. Play it as if you were in the character's core situation but use your own emotions, reactions and words. Take the risk of giving your fullest expressive self to each moment: The *Divine Normal.* Catch and follow your impulses.

6. **When the improvisation is over, ask questions:**

   A. How did the circumstances of the scene we created differ or parallel the scene's circumstances?

   B. How was I different from, or similar to, the character in the scene?

   C. Did any feelings lead to any actions? Emotions make you want to do things.

   D. Did you have any impulses you didn't follow? Why not? Sometimes we don't follow our instincts because we feel they are inappropriate to the scene or to the character. But remember, in this improvisation you are not here to fulfill what you think are the demands of the material. You are here to discover *your* deepest personal responses to the circumstances created by the writer as if they were happening to you. You are *not* the character and do *not* have to do what he or she does. In your exploration you are not bound by the character nor by the circumstances other than the core one you are playing. Take advantage of this freedom.

7. **Read the scene again to absorb more of the circumstances.** This is a critical step. It is amazing how much of a scene eludes us until we explore it in this way. What we read and what actually penetrates us are two different things.

8. **Read the whole of the material again.** We can easily forget the connection between events when we focus on a single scene in detail.

CHAPTER 5

Judging and Valuing

By the way, the teacher asks, how do you know that Krogstad plans to blackmail Nora in this scene if he is forced to?

This stops me in my tracks. I just know he does, is my feeble reply. But before he can tell me to, I read the scene again. It only takes a few minutes and I'm learning to do this almost automatically now. Diane is looking too. I find it!

We know this plan is on his mind because he has the loan agreement with him:

KROGSTAD: Your father died on the twenty-ninth of September. But look at this. Here your father has dated his signature "October 2nd." Isn't that odd, Mrs. Helmer?

From the way he's talking, I observe, he seems to have the paper in his hands with her forged signature on it.

Correct, the teacher says. But, the teacher asks, when did he get it? Does he just happen to carry it around with him every day? Not very likely, I reply. So, presses the teacher, when did he get it? The answer is not in this scene, I say. But we do know that earlier he has been at the Helmer house. He comes to see if rumors about his being fired from his bank job are true. The teacher asks how long ago that was. I need to look at the scenes before the one we are working on, so I grab the play and go back a little. While I'm searching Diane pipes up.

If I saw that paper, says Diane, with my father's forged signature on it, I would want it back so much. It is the one thing that could hang me. And I'm in the same room with it. It's maybe only a few inches away from me. If I could grab it and tear it up, then it would be my word against Krogstad's and I'd be sure to win that! Her voice is excited and her eyes are gleaming.

So, asks the teacher, what is the object of your desire? To tear up that agreement, shouts Diane. Good, says the teacher, so what keeps you from doing it? Well, answers Diane thoughtfully, I still don't know if he even knows about the forgery. I will incriminate myself if I make a move for it. It will certainly arouse his suspicions. Quite a wonderful moment, says the teacher. Diane nods her head, staring out as if seeing the life altering piece of paper right in front of her.

I've found it! Diane and the teacher both look at me. Krogstad left the Helmer house with the bad news of his firing only a short time ago, maybe half an hour or so. We know that he sees Helmer and Mrs. Linde walk past Olsen's restaurant and quite soon after that he is back at the Helmer house.

So, asks the teacher, Krogstad got bad news and went to a restaurant? Sure, I reply. He probably needs to sit down and this place must be near the Helmer house.

And what is he doing at Olsen's restaurant?

That's not in the play, I reply, we don't know. So let's explore it, the teacher says. He puts a table in the corner of the room, tells Diane she is a waitress and tells me to come into "Olsen's."

Another improvisation, I say to myself. Well, this could be fun actually. I immediately think of where I've just been.

I was in Torvald Helmer's office asking if rumors of my firing are true. When he tells me that they are, I plead with him. Even though this scene isn't in the play either, Dr. Rank tells Nora and Mrs. Linde that he overhears me saying that I have to live also. So I am coming into Olsen's a bit stunned, I think. At least that's how I am after I get bad news. So I enter slowly, with my mind clearly on matters other than food. The place is small and pretty empty. I take a seat at a corner table.

Diane comes over and asks me what I'll have. I look at her blankly. I'm really here just to gather myself. I need to think. My legs feel wobbly. But I absently order a cup of coffee. The warmth of it will feel good after the coldness of the outside and the coldness of Torvald Helmer. The teacher asks me to voice my thoughts out loud:

How could he do this to me? What am I going to do? At Christmas time! What a thing to do when he knows I have two children. God! Where else can I get a job? Nobody will even look me in the eyes let alone give me decent work. Sure, kick me again. That's what I'm good for, kicking. God, I hate that man. What am I going to do?

Out of the window I see Torvald Helmer and Christine Linde walking together.

Oh my God. What are they doing together? I did see her with Nora when I came in earlier to talk to Helmer. What is she doing in town? Christine Linde. But is that her? She looks different?

Ten years ago Christine Linde and I were everything to each other. And then, out of the blue, she sends me a letter breaking it all off. I know Nora and she were friends in our old hometown together long ago. Did Christine come into town looking for a job? Did she tell Nora about our old relationship and has Nora engineered my firing so that her friend could have my position? Why else is she walking now with Torvald Helmer?? If that *is* Christine Linde.

They pushed me out! That's what they've done. Nora Helmer has fixed it so that I will be out at the bank and her friend will be in! Can you believe that? She has *never* liked me and after all I did for her, getting her money so that she could save her husband's life. Sure, kick me again.

Well, I'm not just going to lie down and let them walk all over me. If Nora Helmer has so much power over her husband that she can make him do whatever she wants, then I'll use that power to my advantage. They pushed me out. Imagine that. People disgust me.

I get up from my table and head for the door. Where, the teacher asks, are you going? To my place, I reply. I'm going to get the loan document with that woman's forged signature on it and then I'm heading straight back to have a little talk with Nora Helmer. If I need that loan document then I'll damn well use it. The teacher nods his head.

The improvisation is over, but I am rip-roaring ready to head into the scene with Nora. I know where I'm coming from so much better now.

That, says the teacher, was a good exploration. You were able to give voice to Krogstad's thoughts. You were thinking like him. Were you, the teacher asks, *playing* Krogstad?

No, I was playing myself, I reply, but in *his* circumstances. I felt stunned at first, then found that my mind was racing back and forth between my disbelief at what had just happened and trying to figure out what to do next. It seemed like the essence of a kind of quiet panic.

Then when I saw Christine Linde and Torvald Helmer together I felt the outrage of a double betrayal. Helmer has just fired me and Christine, the woman I loved, had just conspired with Nora Helmer to take over my position. I was just beside myself.

Improvising scenes that are implied by the text, says the teacher, but that are not actually spelled out by the writer, is one of the most valuable tools we have as actors for exploring a part.

But now the teacher asks an unexpected question. He asks me what I think of Krogstad. Well, I answer, I have a lot of thoughts about Krogstad. Judge him, the teacher says.

Judge him? I've always been taught *never* to judge a character and I tell the teacher this. He nods his head and agrees with me. Yes, he says we must never judge a character, but we always do. So let's get it out on the table. Go ahead, judge Krogstad, he urges me. Diane and I are just sort of staring at him.

Let me explain, the teacher says. We have feelings about the characters we play, we make judgments about them. Sometimes very negative judgments. And it all goes on just below the surface. We push these opinions away because we think them inappropriate. Acting teachers have jumped down our throats for judging the characters we play. And what they say is true. We cannot truly play a character for whom we do not feel love.

But how do we eliminate these conscious and sometimes subconscious judgments from our playing?

First we have to admit to them, bring them out into the open. If we don't, these judgments will sabotage our performance. And the places where the sabotage is deepest is where the character shows the greatest amount of vulnerability. We simply will be unable to find the tears, the pain, the joys of this person we are supposed to be playing because deep down we despise him or her.

So, I ask you again, what do you think of Krogstad?

After a moment, I decide to tell the truth. I think he's a jerk, I answer, but he's kind of been forced to be. The teacher wants to know why I think Krogstad's a jerk? Well, in the first place, he sleazes his way through some shady crime he commits involving forgery, and then he threatens to blackmail a woman who has never done him any harm. Well, he thinks now that she *has* harmed him because of the job, but he could just ask for her help without threatening her. Frankly, I think he's a bitter, vengeful, twisted little man.

Good, says the teacher, "frankly" is exactly what I'm looking for. And by the way, did you know that "Krogstad" in Norwegian actually means something crooked or twisted? No, I confess, I didn't. But I am secretly pleased with myself.

Now he asks Diane what she thinks of Nora. Diane has a lot to say.

Nora is a superficial, selfish, manipulative liar. She lies to nearly everyone in the play, acts like a sexual plaything towards her husband so she can get whatever she wants from him, plays games with Dr. Rank and is spiteful to her friend Christine; bragging about how great everything is for her and how good she looks. And to top it all off, she walks out on everyone including her children to go out and "find herself." I'm sorry, finishes Diane, I just don't like her at all.

Neither of you likes your character? asks the teacher. We nod our heads. OK, he says, let's see what we can do about this. He looks at Diane and asks her if she herself felt manipulative or superficial in the improvised scene she played with me. No, she says, I never felt like that during the scene. The teacher wonders why not. I felt, Diane says, like the victim in that scene. Here was an old lover putting me in a very awkward situation and then threatening me with the exposure of a potentially very damaging secret. If anything, *I* felt like the one being manipulated.

So, asks the teacher, your opinions of Nora are not based on the scene in question? Well no, Diane says, not really. In her scene with Krogstad, Nora is the victim of his treachery just as I was the victim of Steven's in our improv. So my opinion of her is based more on the other scenes in the play. I mean she plays up her looks so much in the play, it's disgusting. I just can't stand that kind of woman, one who plays games all the time.

I wonder how she got that way, muses the teacher. It seems, answers Diane, that she just went from her father's house straight to Torvald's. I mean she has no real life experience. She's just been taken care of by men all of her life. By *two* men really, her father and her husband. And so she's learned how to manipulate men to get her way. It's all she knows.

But, says the teacher, she's stronger than you isn't she? What, bristles Diane, do you mean? You caved in to the pressure in your improv, explains the teacher, but Nora fights Krogstad off. Diane puts her head down for a second and then agrees that what the teacher says is true. Nora does stand up to Krogstad.

And what, asks the teacher, is her secret anyway?

Nora took out an illegal loan, says Diane, and forged her father's signature on a loan document. Those are her two big secrets.

But why did she do these things?

Well, Diane says, she needed the money for a trip South to Italy because the climate there could save her husband's life. And she forged her father's signature because he was so sick she didn't want to explain to him about Torvald's fragile health for fear it would make him worse.

Doesn't sound very selfish to me, observes the teacher. True, says Diane. And she did those things, continues the teacher, eight years before the scene in question. Also true, admits Diane.

What, asks the teacher all of a sudden, are her values? I'm not sure what you mean, says Diane.

What are her assumptions about the world? asks the teacher; the things she doesn't even think about but just unquestioningly believes?

Diane thinks for a few moments. Nora believes that if you have a good reason for doing something then it is all right to do it even if it has been forbidden or is against the law.

What does she do that is forbidden?

Torvald, answers Diane, forbids her to eat macaroons. But Nora obviously isn't convinced of the correctness of this rule and so, when he isn't looking, she goes right ahead and sneaks some. And when she thinks she has good reason, she borrows money without her husband's permission and forges her father's signature on the loan paper.

The teacher is looking at Diane now and asks her a simple question: Would you?

Would I what?

Would you take out an illegal loan and forge your father's signature if the man you loved was dying and you couldn't get the money that would save his life any other way?

I don't know, answers Diane. If I was in that situation, she says slowly, I guess, at least I hope, I would.

What's another assumption, asks the teacher, that Nora has about the world, about relationships?

That's easy, says Diane, that to keep a man you have to look pretty and give in to what he wants. And I just hate that!

I mean I see where you've been leading me with this values stuff, and I do now start to see her as braver and more devoted to the ones she loves than I did before but...the teacher cuts her off.

That's another assumption or value she has about the world, the teacher says. For Nora, the people she loves are the only ones worth caring about. Strangers can be disregarded. Remember, she tells Torvald not to worry what other people might think if they couldn't pay back a loan. She actually says, "Who cares about them? They're only strangers." And, when Krogstad asks her, "But didn't it occur to you that you were committing a fraud against me?" she answers him with, "I couldn't worry about that. I certainly wasn't concerned about you." It's Torvald and her father that are on her mind, not someone outside her immediate circle.

Yes, says Diane, I see that, but I still can't stand the part of her that plays games with men!

You said yourself, says the teacher, that she has been sheltered all her life, going straight from her father's house to her husband's. Everyone throughout the play from Torvald to Christine Linde to Dr. Rank says she knows little about "the world," the teacher continues. If you had been raised like that, how would you get along?

Christine says that she would have gone to school in the evenings, read books and educated herself. Good, says the teacher. But what if you lived in a time and place where such options were not open to you? What if you knew there was a great big world out there that could have tremendous power over you but over which you could have very little? How would you feel?

Inside, admits Christine, I'd be scared to death. The only world over which I could exercise any control would be my family life then. So I would concentrate all my energies on that. So I guess I would be forced to use the sexual power I have over my husband since that would be the only kind of power I had.

But the question is, the teacher prods, is Nora forced to or does she like to use that power?

Christine thinks for a moment. Both, she says. In the play Nora seems to like using her sexuality. And, asks the teacher, is it a game she plays, the kind of game you hate so much? Yes, replies Christine, I think it is. And sometimes, asks the teacher, games can be fun, yes? Christine nods her head. And sometimes flirting can be fun, right?

But, replies Christine, flirting just to get what you want, to manipulate someone, is not good. But, asks the teacher, has it occurred to you that she might be flirting with her husband because she actually likes him? Christine hesitates. In fact, continues the teacher, don't you find Nora kind of playful anyway? Remember her playing hide-and-seek with her children just before this scene with Krogstad? In fact we hear a lot about her cheerfulness throughout the early parts of the play. She is singing, dancing, bringing Christmas presents, decorating the tree. Why, asks teacher, is she so cheery?

Well, says Christine, that brings us back to the circumstances, which I think is part of this technique you are trying to teach us. All of these questions keep bringing us back to the text and to our personal responses to it. So, let me think.

Last Christmas, things were not so good at the Helmer house. Three weeks before the holiday, Nora worked every evening until well past midnight making flowers to put on the tree and to make special presents for everyone. Before that she has had to take on extra work sewing, doing embroidery and she also got a big copying job last winter. In fact, she had to work hard in order to have enough to make her monthly payments to Krogstad without Helmer finding out about it. Nora likes fine clothes but has had to do with simple things.

Has, the teacher asks, she complained about her less than opulent life style? Diane thinks for a moment. No, I don't think so. I think her basic, what can I call it, *trusting* nature feels that things will work out.

Is, the teacher asks, she having a vital, loving relationship with her husband?

Are you asking me if they are sexually active during all this time?

Yes.

I think, says Diane, that they are. And the reason I say this is how shocked she acts when her friend Christine Linde tells her that she was in a *loveless* marriage herself. Nora acts like she has never heard of such a thing. So she and Helmer are probably doing all right in that department.

Why, asks the teacher, getting back to the point, does Nora accept so much material deprivation? Why has she taken on so much work? Is it because she is a superficial tease?

Nora, replies Diane, is not superficial. She is actually pretty bold. To save her husband's life, she is willing to do whatever she can. I hope I would do the same for my husband. She takes risks for him. And now, it is all turning around.

This Christmas is different. Torvald's new job means that they have money for real Christmas gifts, and that she will finally be able to finish paying off Krogstad. Imagine the relief! So of course she's flying around the house.

There's another reason as well, says the teacher. Do you know what it is? After a moment, Diane shakes her head.

Just before her scene with Krogstad, says the teacher, Nora has found out from Dr. Rank that the dreaded Krogstad works at the bank and is now an employee of her husband's. She finally has some power over this man whom she has feared for years.

Do you, the teacher asks Diane, still hate the kind of woman that Nora is?

No, says Diane, I don't. She loves life, loves her husband, is afraid of what the "world" is, and even though she likes clothes and dancing and fun she is strong, committed and intensely moral.

Moral? asks the teacher. Why do you say that?

She is in desperate need of money, answers Diane, and could get it from her friend Dr. Rank. And I mean she needs it badly, thinking that paying off Krogstad will make him go away. But when she finds out that Rank has been secretly in love with her for years, she cannot take advantage of his feelings and so, she doesn't ask for his help. When it comes right down to it, she cannot do what she feels is wrong.

In fact, now that I think about it, she is far more moral than Helmer is. He *talks* about the moral faults of other people, but when the pressure is on *him*, he gives in right away. At the end of the play he's willing to comply with any demand Krogstad might make in order to avoid a scandal.

Nora thinks throughout the whole play that her husband Torvald will take all the blame on himself and stand up for her, in fact she calls this the "miracle" that is going to happen, but he does the opposite. *He's* the weak one, for all his righteous lectures.

So, asks the teacher, what is one of her values? Something she doesn't question or think about every day but just assumes?

That you don't hurt the ones you care for, answers Diane. And, continues Diane, it even goes beyond that. She believes that the people who care for her will act as she does. I mean she is just so sure that Torvald will act nobly, like she would, and that distresses her to no end. The idea that he would take on to himself her misdeeds is what leads her to consider suicide so seriously. She wouldn't be able to stand seeing him suffer for what *she* did.

You know, says the teacher, she doesn't seem so superficial to me.

She isn't superficial, says Diane, she's a very good person really.

Then what about, asks the teacher, leaving her children? How do you deal with that?

That, says Diane, is a tough one. I think that having her whole world turn upside down so suddenly and completely has made her feel that it would be impossible for her to properly care for her children. And she knows that the woman that raised her, Anne-Marie, will be in the house to tend to them. But yes, this is the toughest part of the role really. For me anyway. I'm still thinking about this.

Well, says the teacher, you've changed some of your feelings about Nora, haven't you?

Yes, well, I guess I have because right now I love her!

Then I guess, says the teacher turning to me, it's time to deal with the bitter, vengeful, twisted little man in the scene.

Krogstad, I say. The teacher nods his head, and asks me to judge the character.

Well, Nils Krogstad screws up this woman's life. Nora's I mean. He must have suspected a long time ago that the loan document Nora turned over to him years before was phony. And I think he's been holding on to it just in case it might someday serve some underhanded purpose of his. And that makes me dislike him. He also feels slimy. I mean the way he is so polite when he comes into this first scene with Nora, it's just creepy.

But I thought that when you did the improvisation in the restaurant, you had some sympathetic feeling for Krogstad?

Yes, I answer, that is true. But that politeness is very weird. I don't think I'd be that way.

When you came in to your scene with Diane, the teacher asks, weren't you polite?

Yes, I admit, I was.

We'll leave that moment alone for now. I'm not trying to get you to play the entrance in any particular way, I'm just trying to leave your choices open.

Plus, I push on, he is threatening to her in the scene. He says, "It's up to you how much Christmas cheer you'll have." And, "If it becomes necessary, I'll fight to the death for my little job at the bank." And, "If I get thrown down a second time, you're coming with me." This is pretty ugly stuff.

Have you, asks the teacher, ever been ugly?

I don't say anything.

Have you ever, he presses, acted or wanted to act vengefully against anyone?

Of course I have, I say.

And you had good reasons for such ugly feelings didn't you?

Yes, I admit, I did.

But you don't want to appear "ugly" in this way in front of other people on stage or on camera, do you?

I admit that I don't. But I defend myself. Krogstad, I say, is a criminal. I mean he committed the crime of forgery himself. There isn't much to like about this guy, I conclude.

No doubt, agrees the teacher. When he agrees with me I always feel a little uneasy.

How, asks the teacher, did Krogstad's relationship with Christine Linde end?

It takes me a second and then I remember. Christine Linde sent him a cruel letter, I say, breaking off the connection between them. It was probably very matter of fact because she says in a later scene that it was her duty to "stamp out" his feelings for her.

And, asks the teacher, what effect did this break-up have on Krogstad?

He was devastated, I reply. He seemed to be counting on her to become his wife. This letter must have come out of the blue and it must have killed him inside. She was basically saying that she didn't love him anymore, probably said that she never had, and was going to marry a man who had more money than he did.

After receiving this letter he moves away from the town where he and Christine lived and comes to the town where Torvald Helmer lives. He can't even stand to be in the same town with Christine. The pain is too much.

Has anyone ever broken your heart?

Yes, I answer.

And what, probes the teacher, happens to Krogstad in his new town?

He must have practiced as a lawyer, but got himself into a situation where he forged someone's signature and was caught. He then used his knowledge as a lawyer to squirm out of a trial but in the process ruined his reputation.

Have you, asks the teacher, ever made a mistake you were caught for? Have you ever lost anyone's trust?

I have, I answer, lost someone's trust in my life, but have never been in the same kind of trouble as Krogstad.

Can you imagine, he asks, such trouble?

Yes, I can, I answer.

What does Krogstad do then?

Well, he has to live. So, he tries to get work in town but finds that no one will employ him. His behavior in keeping his crime out of court has disgusted everyone and they will have nothing to do with him.

But, as I say, he has to live. So, he goes into the shady business of securing loans for people outside of the normal system. And I think in this way he makes himself even more hated. People owe him money and he probably charges a higher interest rate than a regular bank would, but not so much as some. He seems to take some pride in saying that he "has been far from the worst in that line of work." He probably could have gouged people more, but he didn't. He really has to do this stuff, he has two children to care for.

And what, asks the teacher, is the opinion of the people around him?

Dr. Rank, I think, sums it up pretty well when he says to Nora and Christine, "his character, my ladies, is rotten right down to the roots."

What does he say in his head, the teacher wonders, when he notices people looking at him when he walks down the street?

He's thinking, "I know what you all think of me. You say to yourselves oh there goes that disgusting Krogstad, he makes me sick. I would never invite him into my house or be seen talking with him. He's making money from other people's desperation." He probably, I say, feels like a leper.

And then, asks the teacher, what happens for him?

By some incredible stroke of luck, he gets a legitimate job in the town bank. A low level clerking job, I admit, but a real job nonetheless.

Does he make ends meet, asks the teacher, by keeping up his shady loan business?

No, I reply, actually he doesn't. When he gets even the smallest of chances to work in a respectable job, he takes it and abandons the other business.

Can you, wonders the teacher, derive one of Krogstad's values from what you've said so far?

That you have to do what you have to in order to survive.

Do you find that value, asks the teacher, offensive?

I think for a second before saying that, when push comes to shove, I would have to embrace such a value myself.

Good, replies the teacher. Then he asks what happens to Krogstad next.

Well, I say, he continues to collect money from people who owe him but makes no new loans, and continues working at the bank, hoping to work his way back to respectability.

But then a terrible thing happens to him. He hears that Torvald Helmer has been appointed the new bank Manager and that he may be making some changes in the bank staff. He is, of course, extremely concerned for his position, so he does an extraordinary thing. On Christmas Eve he goes to Torvald's house to find out if the rumor of his being replaced is true. And unfortunately discovers that he *will* be replaced after the first of the year. He apparently pleads with Torvald because Dr. Rank hears him say that he has to "*live.*"

So, says the teacher, Krogstad is kicked again.

Yes, I agree, it *is* like he's a dog that just keeps getting kicked. Christine dumps him, the town turns their back on him and he loses the only job he could get. This must be the lowest point of his life. I think that one of his assumptions about the world is that people kick you when you are down, because that is his experience.

Do you feel, asks the teacher, any more sympathy for him than you did before?

I do, I say. Talking about what he has gone through has increased my feeling for him. He acts the way he does because circumstances have forced him to. If I had been through what he has, I might be forced to do many of the same things.

Remember, adds the teacher, that when someone finally shows

some genuine faith in him, he tries to undo the harm he has threatened Nora with.

You mean, I ask, with Christine? He nods his head. That's right, I remember now that when Christine finally convinces him that she wants to be with him, he tries to take back the incriminating letter he has written before Torvald can read it.

He isn't, I say, a bad man. He's basically a good man who has to survive however he can. If you get beaten enough times, you learn to snarl. The teacher is smiling.

I even, I tell him, know what it feels like to act in ways that I don't approve of, to do things where you don't even recognize yourself. And to dislike yourself for your own behavior. I tell the teacher that I think Krogstad is like that.

You both, the teacher summarizes, have come some real distance toward the characters you are playing. By honestly and freely judging them negatively, you put your preconceptions and prejudices on the table so that you could see them.

After voicing your real feelings about the characters you then looked at their values, their circumstances, and tried to get a feel for *why they are the way they are*. And then you asked yourselves if you had ever or *could* ever feel like they do. In this way you are working deeply on the characters even though you don't realize it.

Inside of you emotions are shifting and aligning themselves in sympathy with the characters in the play. It is the magical inner movement of empathy. Without trying to *become* Nora or Krogstad, you are nonetheless building emotional bridges to them. If you had to defend them in a court of law, you could do it with passion. And in a way, that is what actors do; become passionate advocates for the characters they play.

Judging a character is clearly something you can do at home without a scene partner. After reading the material, judgments will have crept into your mind no matter how hard you've tried to keep them out. This is natural and even good. You must have opinions and feelings about the characters.

After your first improvisation make a list of the negative feelings you have about your character. Be brutally honest. Hold nothing back. If you truly have no negative judgments of the character, which is a rarity (even a hero can be nauseatingly perfect), you can move on to the next step.

That next step is to look at *why* the character is the way they are. This means looking more closely at their circumstances. Make a list of the assumptions they have about the world, the things they don't question or think about but just assume. Rephrasing the Golden Rule can be helpful here. For example one character's Golden Rule, or assumption about how the world works could be, "Do unto others before they do it to you."

You could go further and use the character typology created by Moni Yakim[1] and try to determine if you think your character is dominated by one of the following "selves": The Vulnerable self, the Instinctive self, the Social self, the Trusting self, the Unresolved self or the Decisive self. Yakim feels that Nora is dominated by the Trusting self. Deep down she believes that everything will turn out all right. She unquestioningly believes that Torvald is truly the noble being that she thinks he is.

Because we cannot fully play a character we do not love, this step is a crucial one. It helps us to see how we feel about

---

[1]From his excellent book *Creating A Character*, published by Applause Books. These "selves" are defined in detail there. An example of a character dominated by the Vulnerable self would be Blanche in *Streetcar Named Desire*; the Instinctive self would be Stanley, also in *Streetcar;* a character dominated by the Social self would be Iago (a character wearing a mask); the unresolved self would be Hamlet; and dominated by the decisive self would be Shakespeare's Henry V.

out characters and then helps us find ways to dispel our judgments and replace them with our empathy.

Suppose you must play Adolph Hitler. Not an easy task unless you want to play him at every moment shouting and raising his arm. But how does he play with children, with his dog? Did you know he *loved* dogs and children? How do you reconcile this with a "monster"?

You must see him from his point of view. Hitler did not often think of himself as a monster, if he ever did. He thought of himself as a savior. He felt he was forced to do some of the terrible things he did because he had to save the German people and the "superior" races. Let the *audience* judge his behavior as monstrous.

PROCESS REVIEW

9. **Judge the characters.** Try to identify all the negative feelings and opinions you have about the character and say them out loud. Judgments keep us away from the character and keep us from giving ourselves over to them wholeheartedly. Admitting them early in the process gives us a chance to get rid of them and to empathize with the character. We cannot play a character we do not love. Sometimes we tell ourselves that we really like the characters even though we are holding on to secret judgments of them. This can be a most dangerous and insidious kind of self-deception. Be careful.

10. **Examine why the character is the way she is.** Look at the character's assumptions about the world and ask how they acquired these assumptions. This will force you to look more carefully at each character's circumstances. Then ask yourself if you were in the same circumstances as the character whether you might act as they have. If you can see life from your character's point of view, then you are on your way to becoming a passionate advocate for them and will show their story without prejudice.

CHAPTER 6

Adding In

A second improvisation? I feel ready to tackle the scene as Ibsen wrote it, I think. I read through the scene again and realize that I still feel a little overwhelmed by parts of it. But I do wonder when we get to Ibsen's circumstances and Ibsen's lines. So I ask.

Later, is the teacher's reply. At first learning this way of working can seem slow, he explains, but the more familiar you become with using it, the faster it can be employed.

A major part of this process, he says, lies in bouncing between *experiencing* the circumstances of the play as ourselves, and talking about and *analyzing* it afterwards. Experience, then analysis. In this way your analysis is the result of your experience.

The next improvisation will include more than just the blackmail. This time you will explore, *as yourselves*, the blackmail and one or two other central circumstances from the scene.

What, asks the teacher, are the most important circumstances besides the blackmail itself?

Diane and I both think. She says that a central circumstance for her is that Nora does what she does for a loved one and not for herself. I say that it is central that Krogstad is going to lose his job and that he thinks Nora is to blame.

The teacher has an idea as well. He says that the next most important circumstance to him is that there is a secret loan between these two people and that there is a forged loan document.

Can you, the teacher then asks, construct a scenario that will incorporate these elements?

Diane and I try to come up with something. We decide on the following idea: Diane's husband has contracted the AIDS virus. They are keeping this fact secret because they are afraid that he will lose his job if the firm he works for finds out. They have a health insurance policy that they fear will not be renewed if the insurance company finds out about his condition. Some of the drugs they need are too expensive to pay for privately, but they don't want to put in an insurance claim. Diane finds out about a man who makes loans and goes to him for the money to buy the drugs her husband needs. She tells her husband that the money is coming from her mother and even though he doesn't like it, he accepts it.

The man who loans her the money, we decide, works for Diane's husband but has been fired by him. He goes to Diane, who he thinks is behind his firing, to ask her to help him get his job back. When she refuses, he tells her he knows about her husband's disease and will tell the company about it if she won't help him. He also has gotten hold of the health insurance contract with both of their signatures on it that misrepresents the husband's condition.

These circumstances follow Ibsen's in far closer detail than our first improvisation did and we wonder if we're taking on too much.

That is a danger, says the teacher. But let's see how you do.

Diane and I set up a simple living room and give it a go.

Diane begins by watching TV and switching channels. I knock at the door, but the TV is too loud for her to hear me, so I open the door.

STEVEN: Uh, excuse me.
DIANE: *(Startled.)* What...what are you doing here?
STEVEN: I'm sorry, I didn't mean to scare you, I knocked but I guess you couldn't hear me, and the door was open...
DIANE: I'm sorry, but you can't just come barging in here...what do you want, what are you doing here?
STEVEN: I just want to talk to you.
DIANE: Look, I pay you the monthly installments, don't I?
STEVEN: Yes, yes you do.
DIANE: If you're here for another payment, it isn't time and I don't have enough right now...
STEVEN: I'm not here about the money. May I come in?
DIANE: Well, just for a moment.
STEVEN: You know that your husband intends to fire me by the end of the month?
DIANE: No, I didn't know that.
STEVEN: Well he told me so himself just a few hours ago.
DIANE: Well, I'm sorry to hear that.
STEVEN: I hope that's true.
DIANE: Maybe it's for the best. I mean maybe you could get a better job elsewhere.
STEVEN: I want to keep the job I have.
DIANE: Look, I don't know what you want me to do. It seems a little late to get your job back don't you think?
STEVEN: The reason I'm here is to ask you if you will try to talk your husband into keeping me on.
DIANE: I don't see how I can do that. I have nothing to do with his business.
STEVEN: May I sit down?
DIANE: I really don't have time for this discussion.
STEVEN: This looks comfortable. *(He sits.)*
DIANE: I'm sorry but I'll have to ask you to go.

STEVEN: You know what I think? I think you're so antsy because you never told your husband about the loan you took from me.

DIANE: I did what I had to do. We needed money for medication.

STEVEN: And you couldn't get it from your medical plan?

DIANE: That really is none of your business.

STEVEN: But it is my business, that's the whole point. I did you a favor getting you that money, now I'm asking you to do a favor for me.

DIANE: A favor? You get plenty off that loan with the interest you charge. You didn't do it for me, you did it for yourself. It was a straight business deal.

STEVEN: I'll ask you again if you'll talk to your husband for me.

DIANE: I don't have any influence over him in that kind of thing.

STEVEN: So you're saying you won't help me?

DIANE: I wish you wouldn't keep persisting in this. I'm sorry you lost your job, but my husband must have had good reason to let you go and I'm not going to interfere. I'm sorry, but that's it. Now I'll have to ask you to go.

STEVEN: *(Not moving.)* If you don't help me, I'll tell him.

DIANE: Tell him what?

STEVEN: About the loan.

DIANE: Why would you do that to me?

STEVEN: Do you think I want to? I don't. But I need this job. If you don't help me with your husband, I'll tell him about the loan.

DIANE: Think about what you're doing. Come on. This is like out of a Mafia movie or something.

STEVEN: This is not a movie. I'm serious. If you don't help me I'll do what I have to do.

DIANE: Fine, you tell him. In the end he'll just hate you and forgive me.

STEVEN: Maybe. Maybe you're right. Do you want to risk it?

DIANE: Yes. Now please get out of my house.

STEVEN: Look, I really don't want to do this, but if I have to I will.

DIANE: Do what?
STEVEN: I know why you needed that money.
DIANE: Yes, for medication. I told you.
STEVEN: Your husband is HIV positive, Mrs. Cloud. You and he tried to hide it, but I did a little digging and found out. I even got a copy of the health insurance form where you lie about his condition.
DIANE: *(Tears well up in her eyes.)* You get out of my house. How dare you? What is the matter with you, using something like this against someone? It's sick.
STEVEN: I have good reasons, Mrs. Cloud, for what I do. So you go right ahead and call me all the names you want, but unless you help me, I will let it be known around here that your husband is infected with the AIDS virus, and that you both lied about his condition on your health insurance forms.
DIANE: He never even saw those forms. He didn't know anything about that.
STEVEN: Really? So you put his name there?
DIANE: What if I did?
STEVEN: It means you falsified a legal document. That's against the law, Mrs. Cloud. You broke the law in a couple of ways, really. First, You didn't disclose your husband's true condition and then you forged his name.
DIANE: Please can't you just leave us alone?
STEVEN: Now I can see that you're upset and I'm sorry about that. And I don't have to do any of this if you'll talk to your husband for me.
DIANE: I don't know what I would say, or even how I would bring up your name. I don't know how to do what you're asking me to do.
STEVEN: But you'll do it?
DIANE: *(Pause.)* Yes, I'll do it. But you have to swear not to say a word about any of this.
STEVEN: If you get me my job back, then I won't have to say or do a single thing.

DIANE: I'm only going to talk to him you know, I can't promise that it will work.

STEVEN: It'll have to, Mrs. Cloud. Because I'm telling you, if I go down, you and your husband are coming with me. *(He exits.)*

We're pretty proud of ourselves because we got in a lot of Ibsen's circumstances. The teacher however looks neither pleased nor *dis*pleased. He looks rather thoughtful in fact.

You got in a lot of Ibsen's circumstances, he begins slowly, but that wasn't the point.

If you become too concerned with getting plot points into your scene at this early stage, then you are focusing on the wrong thing. This improvisation isn't a test to see how much you remember. It is a chance for you to experience the character's basic situation as yourselves. You have greater freedom here than you are allowing yourselves.

Actors have a wonderful but often crippling desire to do what they think is "right." They want to fulfill the demands of the script right away, but when they do this, they miss so many of the seemingly "inappropriate" choices that might, in reality, be closer to the essence of the scene than their preconceived notions of it.

You were "good" little actors in the scene you just played. You were "good" students, doing what you thought would please me; as if I were going to test you on how many of the circumstances you could fit into your improvisation. But this exercise is for *you*, not for me. What did *you* get out of it besides the pride of having mirrored Ibsen's circumstances so well?

Give me actors, the teacher says, who are selfish, who explore for their own enrichment not for mine. You missed the opportunity, because you were concentrating on getting in plot points, of discovering unique and interesting behavior that might flow from your spontaneous reactions to what was unfolding before you. You became talking heads who were mere messengers of the story. But you are not *messengers* of the story, *you are the story!* Your reactions, your behavior *is* the story.

If you bind yourselves too soon to what you think the requirements of the script are, you will find it extremely difficult to find the life of the part in yourselves later on. You will have put yourselves in a prison, a straight jacket from which escape will become more and more impossible just as it becomes more and more desired.

Diane and I are both confused. What the teacher says is probably true, at least it strikes a chord in me, but weren't we *told* to play the circumstances? Aren't we being criticized for what we were *asked* to do? Diane asks for clarification.

Yes, the teacher replies, you *were* asked to create a scene that added in a couple of the most important circumstances from the scene to accompany the core blackmail one. But you both became so focused on making your scene parallel Ibsen's, that you didn't live inside the circumstances as yourselves. And that is the real point here.

Are you saying, asks Diane, that what we did would have been right if we had done it later on in this process you are teaching us?

It is never right, answers the teacher, to leave yourself out of what you are doing. But yes, remembering the events of the scene and the order of their occurrence *is* a later part of this process.

What you need to be concerned with at this point is giving life, your life, to the external circumstances. Stanislavski put it like this: "...the actor is now coming to his part not through the text, the words of his role, nor by intellectual analysis or other conscious means of knowledge, but through his own sensations, his own real emotions, his personal life experience."[1]

---

[1] Stanislavski, Constantine, *Creating A Role*, trans. E.R. Hapgood, Routledge Press, NYC, 1989, p. 25.

Be careful, summarizes the teacher, of getting bogged down too early in trying to load all of the circumstances of the scene onto your improvisation without *experiencing them* as yourselves.

Now we can still use what you did, says the teacher, so let's push on to the next step, which is to read through the scene again.

Diane and I read the scene again. After that, we look expectantly at our teacher. He raises his eyebrows at us. This means we should know without his prompting, what we are to do next. I look at my notes. Now, I say, we ask ourselves three critical questions.

First, I declare, we ask how the circumstances we created differed or paralleled the written scene's.

Diane pipes up. I gave in, she laments. I told Steven I would do what he wanted, but Nora doesn't tell Krogstad that in Ibsen's scene. She resists him to the end. But Steven had so much power over my husband's life, Diane goes on, that I just had to do what he wanted. The teacher nods his head.

What threat, asks the teacher, does Krogstad hold over Nora's head?

Well, says Diane, the death of her relationship with Torvald. In our scene it was the literal death of my husband. If he can't get his medicine, he will die.

Is the death of her relationship with Torvald, asks the teacher, as important to Nora as the physical death of your husband was to you in your improvised scene?

I think it is, replies Diane. Her relationship with Torvald is everything to Nora. She will do almost anything to preserve it.

Then the emotions you felt at the moment of the threat are no different from the ones Nora might feel?

Yes, answers Diane, it's true. For that moment, I was in Nora's emotional world, but as myself. What a horrible position she is in.

Yes, says the teacher, and the audience will feel the terror of it just as you did if you do your job right. The genuineness of your reaction, if properly physicalized, will give the audience a visceral insight into Nora's inner life. *That* is what you are after.

I now have something to say about the circumstances. I have read the scene again, I say, and I now realize that there was no conspiracy between Diane and someone else to have me fired in our improvisation the way there is in Ibsen's scene.

When Krogstad comes in, I continue, he thinks, but isn't yet sure, that Nora and Christine Linde have gotten together to force him out.

Krogstad spends the first part of his scene with Nora making sure that the woman he saw with Torvald Helmer is really Christine Linde, that she is newly arrived in town and that she is an old friend of Nora's.

Do you see, asks the teacher, what is happening? By first experiencing important circumstances from the scene as yourselves, with your own words and without trying to become the characters, you are being driven deeper and deeper into the text.

You are now looking quite carefully at the first moments of Ibsen's scene because they were *not* a part of your improvisation. When you read through the scene again, after your improvisation, those circumstances hit you with a palpable force just *because* they were absent from your scene.

Remember, this is not a test. Circumstances that you leave out are only that. You are not required to get them all in. What is interesting is to see what has stuck and what hasn't.

Now this leads us to a question, says the teacher. He looks straight at me and asks, why is Krogstad, who suspects he has been plotted against, so polite at the beginning of Ibsen's scene? Why isn't he a raving maniac?

He could be, I say. His lines could be said with vicious sarcasm. But a few things argue against that approach. Krogstad isn't sure about the conspiracy he imagines. He only suspects. If he is wrong, he will have made a bad mistake. But I also think that he observes the social respect due his boss's wife.

Which isn't to say, I conclude, that sarcasm isn't a part of his personality.

How did each of you, the teacher asks, differ or parallel the characters?

I was definitely weaker than Nora, says Diane. She somehow withstands his threats. I wilted. But I had a real sense of the desperation that this threat causes. I didn't know what to do, and I think Nora feels the same way at times in Ibsen's scene.

What is the crucial difference, the teacher presses, between you and Nora?

Diane thinks for a moment and then reads through the scene again silently. The teacher and I do the same.

I think, Diane begins, that her faith in Torvald is what gives her the strength to fight off Krogstad's threats. She says that Torvald will see what kind of man Krogstad really is. And she has a kind of faith, that's all I can call it, that even the law will be on her side when all the facts are known. I mean I think part of that is bluff, but she can even *think* of such a bluff because a part of her believes that when you do things for the right reasons everything will turn out. I didn't have that faith in the improvised scene with Steven.

You have hit, says the teacher, on an important aspect of Nora's character. But do you realize how dangerous this insight could be?

Diane shakes her head.

Now that you've decided that Nora has a faith in things turning out all right, you as an actress might not let Krogstad's threat affect you. You might go through the scene saying to yourself, well everything will turn out all right so I won't get too upset about all this. And this will reduce the stakes of the scene for you and consequently, for Nora.

I understand exactly what you mean, says Diane. I must be clearer. This faith is one that she finds *after* her world has been shaken. But we must see that her world *is* shaken. This faith cannot always be in place, because that would render her invulnerable to any sense of danger, or any sense of fear or of despair.

It, corrects the teacher, will render *you* invulnerable to any sense of danger, fear or despair.

Right, says Diane. *Me.*

By the way, asks the teacher, what is on Nora's mind when she realizes that Krogstad is at the door? You've experienced the basic circumstance a couple of times, what do you think is on Nora's mind?

Well, the first thing, answers Diane, is that Krogstad represents a danger here in Nora's house. If Torvald sees them together he will most certainly start asking questions and the whole loan business might come spilling out. I think she would be feeling a great deal of fear and would want Krogstad out of there. I think that's what's on her mind, getting Krogstad to go away.

Does, the teacher asks, the circumstance and the emotion that goes with it lead to an action?

Well, says Diane, the feeling makes me want to go to the door. Not let him into the room. I want to make it clear to him that I am not inviting him into my home. I also don't want the maid or Anne-Marie to hear me talking to this man. I feel paranoid and just want him to leave. Torvald must not see or hear about us being together. It will lead to too many questions.

So why then do you let him in and have an extended conversation with him? the teacher asks.

He seems to have some urgent business with me, explains Diane. And then he makes a kind of veiled threat saying, "It's up to you how much Christmas cheer you'll have." I have to find out what this is all about.

OK, says the teacher, we're getting a little ahead of ourselves but that's all right. Let's get back to our three questions.

Steven, the teacher asks, how were you different from, or similar to, Krogstad?

For one thing, I say, I wasn't as polite as Krogstad. I came in and sat down without being asked. I also got to the point more quickly than he does. Especially when it comes to the second part of his blackmail. He leads Nora through all these lawyer-like questions before he gets to the forgery. It's like he lays a trap for her, and I never did anything like that. And I think Krogstad feels more taken advantage of than I did. When I read the scene again, I start to feel that he is genuinely hurt by what he sees as Nora's betrayal of him. I mean, he got her a loan when she needed it, and she repays him by helping to push him out of his job.

Diane suddenly shouts:

DIANE: I don't even know what you're talking about! Something ignites inside me.

STEVEN: I know what I know! You can deny it all day long but I'm not an idiot. I know that your friend came into town needing a job, TOLD YOU THAT SHE DUMPED PATHETIC ME YEARS AGO, which I'm sure you both had a GOOD LAUGH about, and that you got your husband to fire me and HIRE HER.

DIANE: I don't know WHAT YOU'RE TALKING ABOUT. That is not...

STEVEN: Oh, come off it. WHATEVER. You just fix it. Fix what you did to me. Get your husband to CHANGE HIS MIND. And stop SNICKERING BEHIND MY BACK.

DIANE: I'm not...

STEVEN: Everybody thinks they can kick me and laugh at me and I'm SICK OF IT, SICK OF IT, **SICK OF IT!** You all treat me like I'm some kind of repulsive bug, but you all come to me when you NEED something, don't you? Well you're no better than me, **NONE OF YOU! YOU ALL MAKE ME SICK! AND I'LL GOD DAMN DO WHATEVER I HAVE TO DO TO GET BY!!**

I am huffing and puffing pretty hard. When Diane jumped in I just lost it. The surprise of it set me off. I don't think I've ever been so upset in a scene before. All the words and feelings just came tumbling out.

That, says the teacher, was some of what was missing from

your second improvisation. Good, Steven. You took the circumstances personally, and you let them affect you. I beg you to do that all the time. Both in any improvised scenes you play and in any scripted ones. You *have* to find your personal responses to the circumstances before you have a chance to find the character's responses and make them real.

So your Krogstad feels that everyone is laughing at him behind his back?

I guess so, I admit. I didn't realize it until I said and felt it, but that's the bottom line truth of it.

The bottom line truth is what we're after, says the teacher.

Now, I say, catching my breath, I'm not sure that Krogstad actually *shows* as much anger as I just did, but it sure seems to be there. At least for me.

I'm not sure either, says the teacher. Let's leave actual performance choices for later. Right now we are finding *you* in the *part*. Later the *part* will find it's way into *you*.

Any other differences or similarities, asks the teacher, with the characters?

Yes, says Diane. Nora has just found out that Krogstad is now an employee of her husband's and no longer feels afraid of him, so she flaunts her superiority over him in the scene and I never did or even felt that in the improvisation. She says straight out to Krogstad, "when one is in an inferior position, Mr. Krogstad..." I mean that is just so bold. I never really felt that I had any power over Steven in our second or even our first improvisation.

The teacher seems satisfied with our progress so far and asks us to address the third question. Did feelings lead to any actions?

The truth is, we admit, that in our second improvisation, feelings didn't really lead to any actions. We were so concerned with stuffing the scene with what we could remember of Ibsen's details, that we didn't feel much at all.

Right. You were both so bound up in fulfilling Ibsen's scene that you did violence to it. You did not give each moment it's full value and you did not find any unique behavior because you did not let any feelings lead to any actions.

But even though you didn't do the best second improvisation, you did discover a lot about Ibsen's scene and about his characters. By bouncing back and forth between experiencing the circumstances and analyzing the text, you were still able extract some useful things from this exercise.

And although I do not say so out loud because I think the teacher would disapprove, I am starting to feel a little more like Krogstad. Whoever *he* is.

WORKING AT HOME

After judging the character and finding empathy with him or her, set up a situation where you add in two or three more important circumstances from the written scene.

Create a simple set and enter it as yourself. This time you are conforming more closely to the written text but you are still in that circumstance *as yourself*, do not try to play the character. Use your own words. When working alone, you do not need to imagine elaborate dialogue for the other character. Just imagine the main points of contention and let them affect you.

Observe your own behavior. As you imagine, for example, that Krogstad is bringing up the oddity of the signature, you might find yourself worrying your cuticles. A piece of behavior like that could be extremely useful; it is an external action that is worth investigating. Ask yourself why you are doing it. When you do, you may discover that it makes you feel like a guilty child. You may decide that this behavior would be more useful for a moment when *Torvald* is lecturing you. Note it, and try it out later on.

After a thorough exploration, read the scene again and ask yourself, how did my circumstances parallel or differ from the scene's, how was I different from, or similar to the character, and did any feelings lead to any actions?

Write down your discoveries in the script or in a separate journal so that you do not simply trust them to memory.

If discoveries are not too concrete, let the experience bubble and boil inside you. Sometimes, deep down, we are engaged in a mysterious creative turmoil where our feelings and thoughts are mixed and remixed by our imaginative powers and the results don't manifest themselves for several days. Let it be; that struggle is part of the process.

PROCESS REVIEW

11. **Do a second improvisation adding in** one or two more of the most important circumstances to the core circumstance from the first improvisation. Play the circumstances in your own words *as yourself*, your most expressive and reactive self, not as the character. Concentrate on your feelings and reactions NOT on how many plot points you can get in, or in what order they occur.

12. **Read the scripted scene again.**

13. **Ask four questions.**
    A. How did the circumstances in the improvisation parallel or differ from the ones in the written scene? This question is **not a test.** You are using the improvisation to force you back into the text.
    B. How was I similar to or different from the character in the scene?
    C. Did feelings lead to any actions?
    D. Did I have any impulses I didn't follow? Why not?

Use the improvisations to bounce back and forth between experiencing the circumstances and comparing them with the written text.

CHAPTER 7

Listing Events

It is now time, says the teacher, to look at the circumstances in more detail. We are going to divide the scene into smaller "events" and create an order of their occurrence. This sequence of events will be based on your experience of the circumstances in the last two improvisations and on the analysis of the scene you did after each improvisation was over.

We must be careful, the teacher warns, to make our analyses and divisions only *after* we have been down at ground level with the character's basic circumstances; after we have experienced our own feelings and actions in *their* circumstances.

What, asks the teacher, is the first event?

Well, says Diane, I sense a trap here.

The teacher looks at her.

I think, she continues, that the first event is what has been going on *just* before the actual scene begins. The teacher smiles. I thought so, exclaims Diane.

In that case then, she says, the first event for Nora is playing a game of what seems to be hide-and-seek with her children.

Why, wonders the teacher, is she playing with them?

This stops Diane. Because, she says, she wants to.

But why, persists the teacher, does she want to?

Oh, I don't know. Because it's fun? Diane is clearly getting exasperated. Is there something I'm missing here?

If I were playing the part, the teacher says, I would wonder why Nora is playing with her children right at this point in the play. I would wonder if there was some very clear reason.

I'll read the scene before this one to see if there is a reason, says Diane dutifully. She reads and then her eyes light up.

Of course, she says. Not only is it Christmas eve, and not only does Nora finally have some spending money, but she has just gotten her old friend, Christine Linde, a job. But best of all, Nora has just learned that Krogstad is an employee of Torvald's! She is so happy to learn this bit of news that she breaks into laughter, starts humming and passes out the forbidden macaroons.

Playing with her kids is a way of celebrating her release from fear. She has been under Krogstad's thumb for years and suddenly things are reversed! She has some leverage over him! Yes, she's celebrating!

You knew this before, but now it means something not just to your head? asks the teacher.

Yes, answers Diane, I can feel it in my body.

Then, says the teacher, go ahead.

Go ahead, and what?

Play this first event. Play with kids knowing what you know about what Nora has just found out, but play as yourself.

With imaginary kids?

Sure, says the teacher, why not?

Let me see if I understand this. You want me to explore, as myself, Nora's first event. An event that consists of playing hide-and-seek with her, or my, kids. And I'm doing this because I am happy that a huge burden has been removed from my shoulders. Is that right?

The teacher nods his head.

Actually, says Diane, this could be fun.

Diane moves out into the space, sets up a few chairs and tables to be a room and starts to play.

DIANE: All right. Stay out, stay out. Now *(She starts to position herself behind the chairs.)* you have to count to ten before you can come in. *(She is down now out of sight. She calls out.)* OK, YOU CAN START! *(She gets up quickly, having spied a pillow in one corner, and uses it to cover herself. She ducks down behind the chair again. After a short while she peeks out and seems to see little kids looking for her. They clearly have no idea where she is, so she makes a noise. One of the "kids" finds her.)* Oh, you found me! That was very smart of you! Let's do it again and this time mommy will hide better, because you're just too good at finding me. *(Diane looks around for more props. She finds more pillows and some cushions and builds a little cave in which to hide. She is having a great deal of fun.)* OK you guys, now try and find me but make sure you count to ten first! *(She buries herself in her little barricade.)*

I have a devilish impulse and look over at the teacher. He raises his eyebrows at me which I decide means approval, so I scream at the top of my lungs, "**FIRE!**"

Diane jumps out of her hiding place and looks around startled. There is obviously no fire.

DIANE: What the hell did you do that for?

STEVEN: *(Splitting his looks between Diane and the teacher.)* I wanted to give you the experience of having your fun ruined kind of in the same way that Nora's fun is ruined. In the scene I mean.

DIANE: Well, it worked!

Luckily Diane is laughing. She says that she was so caught up in playing the game that she forgot about the rest of the scene completely. And she says further that hearing Krogstad's voice out of the blue the way it is in Ibsen's scene is probably as startling for Nora as it was for her to hear me screaming "fire."

The teacher tells Diane that she has a firm grasp of the first event. He then turns to me and asks what my first event is.

Coming to the door, I answer.

Tell me about coming to the door, says the teacher.

I've been told that I will be officially fired around the first of the year, I've gone to a café to process this, I see my boss and my old lover, Christine Linde, walking together and think that Nora and Christine have probably conspired to push me out of my position at the bank.

That position is the first step in my attempt to win back a place of respect in this town and so I decide to go to Nora and ask her if she'll try to persuade her husband to keep me on at the bank. But just in case she won't, I stop by my place and get the forged loan document. I may not want to use it, but I may be forced to.

Walk me to the door, says the teacher.

OK. I am pretty steamed up thinking about this conspiracy of Nora's and Christine's to shove me out, but I'm not entirely sure if it's true. When I get to the house, the door is part way open.

What are you thinking at that exact moment? asks the teacher.

Instead of answering with words, I go to the door in the room and stand behind it.

I'm having a lot of thoughts and feelings, I say. I don't find it so easy to knock. I am extremely upset and want to scream at Nora. But screaming at her might make her less likely to grant the favor I want from her. Plus, I'm not certain that my suspicions about a female conspiracy against me is actually true.

Plus, it's Christmas eve and I hear her playing with her children. I have children too. I'm going to walk in here and be a bummer, bring bad feelings into her house and I really don't want to do that. But I have to. My official firing is only a week away. I'm forced to be the bad guy once again.

Go ahead and explore this event, says the teacher.

Let me make sure I understand. This event is about a man who has been told he will soon lose a crucial job, comes into his boss's house on Christmas eve, asks the boss's wife, a woman who has a secret loan with him, to use her influence to get her husband to change his mind about firing him?

That's the event, says the teacher.

I go behind the door. As I arrive, I look around to see if Torvald Helmer is on his way back. I don't know how long he'll be away from the house and I don't want him to see me here. I take a deep breath and settle myself down to go through with a task that I really don't want to do. I knock on the door. I wait. There is no response, but the force of the knock has pushed the door open a little further. I poke my head in a ways and hear children's voices. And Nora's. I push the door open enough to come part way in. As I watch the game the kids and Nora are playing, I think of my own kids and how there will be no Christmas fun for them. Daddy is unemployed. This thought makes me bold enough to get on with my business.

STEVEN: Excuse me.
DIANE: *(She gets up to participate in the scene with Steven.)*
DIANE: Mr., Krogs...what are you doing here?
STEVEN: *(Staying by the door.)* I was wondering if I could talk to you for a second?
DIANE: You want to talk to me? Well, uh, go into the other room kids OK, we'll play more in just a little while. Go on. Now what do you want? *(In a quiet voice.)* I won't have the payment until the first of the month.
STEVEN: This isn't about the money.

The teacher stops us. Good, he says, but the first event is over isn't it? Are we into something new now?

We both agree that we are.

So, says the teacher, let's go back. Are there other ways you could come in that door? he asks.

Sure, I say.

There are *fifty* ways, a *hundred* ways, an *infinite* number of ways you could come in that door, the teacher explodes. As you work on the part, explore each event in many ways without deciding or locking any of them down. At this point your job is to open up possibilities, options, choices. Try another way.

I go back behind the door. I have never worked on a part in this way and yet it doesn't feel unfamiliar. In fact I think I have unconsciously worked this way all of my performing life without really realizing it. This process is one I have explored while daydreaming or while washing dishes. What is so exciting is to have it spelled out consciously. Exploring this way ignites my creative imagination.

This time when I get to the door, I am hopping mad. I can barely contain the rage I feel at Nora for betraying me. That's how I feel. I saved her husband's life with a loan and she pays me back by getting her husband to give her old friend my old job! I'm going to stick her and stick her good.

I knock, wait a few seconds, then knock again louder. I step through the doorway and watch Nora play with her kids. I can't wait to spoil her fun.

STEVEN: Excuse me Mrs. Helmer, I see you're busy right now but maybe you could spare me a little of your *precious* time.

The teacher stops me. That, he says, is another good exploration of the first event. At home you could and should do many more explorations of just this single event. We would do it here, but I want to move on to the next steps.

We are going to list the major events of the scene. These events will give us the contour, the shape of the scene, and our improvisations will now attempt to follow that contour, that pattern.

We are honing in, closing in, on Ibsen's circumstances bit by bit and as we do so, we will continue to use our own feelings, words and selves. Do not memorize any lines, or try to play a character, or play only emotions that you think are "appropriate." As we list these events, let's try to frame them as actions.

What is the first event of the scene? asks the teacher. For Diane we have decided that it is playing hide-and-seek with her children. Playing with children is an action, so we will accept this as Nora/Diane's first event. For Steven we have decided that the first event is coming to the door and stepping part way in. This too is an action and so we like it as a first event for Steven/Krogstad.

What *feels* like the next large event?

Diane and I both look at the scene. I say that Krogstad's next big event is to get some time with Nora. Diane says that her next big event is to find out what Krogstad wants.

And what lines of dialogue does this next event cover? asks the teacher.

We say that the event encompasses these lines of dialogue:

KROGSTAD: I beg your pardon, Mrs. Helmer.

NORA: (*Turns, with a stifled cry, half jumps up.*) Ah! What do you want?

KROGSTAD: Excuse me. The front door was open—somebody must have forgotten to shut it.

NORA: (*Rising.*) My husband's not here, Mr. Krogstad.

KROGSTAD: I know that.

NORA: Well—what do you want?

KROGSTAD: A word with you.

NORA: With—? (*To the children, quietly.*) Go in with Anne-Marie. No the strange man won't hurt mama. When he's gone we can play some more. (*She leads the children in to the room on the left and closes the door after them. Now tense and nervous.*) You want to speak with me?

KROGSTAD: Yes I do.

NORA: Today—? But it's not the first of the month yet—

KROGSTAD: No, it's Christmas eve. It's up to you how much Christmas cheer you'll have.

NORA: What so you want? Today I can't possibly—

KROGSTAD: We won't talk about that right now. It's something else. I suppose you have a moment?

NORA: Well, yes; all right, though—
KROGSTAD: Good.

That dialogue, we say, covers the second event.

What do you want to call that event? asks the teacher.

Diane calls it, *Finding out* and writes it by that section of dialogue.

I call it, *Getting her to talk* and write that in my script by those lines.

As you see, says the teacher, some of your events will be different and some will be the same. It is a good idea to do as you are doing, to write them down from *your* character's point of view.

He asks Diane to show him her list, which she has made on a separate sheet of paper. It looks like this.

1) Play with the kids.
2) Find out what Krogstad wants.

Good, says the teacher. But let's also connect these events one to the other. So let's add the trigger that changes one event into another. What triggers your second event? he asks Diane.

Well, Krogstad comes in.

Right. So how could you notate that on your list?

Diane shows him her amended list:

1) Play with the kids.
   Krogstad comes in and interrupts.
2) Find out what Krogstad wants.

The teacher nods his head at her list. Of course, he says, we could consider Krogstad's entrance as a separate event and that would be fine. But since we are trying to get at the largest events let's leave it the way it is.

How have you listed the events so far, Steven?

I show him my list:

1) Come in the door.
2) Get time with her.

By the way, what do you have to do to secure her attention?

Well, I have to kind of threaten her with that stuff about a cheerful Christmas before she'll give me the attention I came for. Soon after that she says she has a moment for me.

Right. Now what is the next large event?

Diane and I read ahead in the script. I say that the next event is Krogstad finding out about Christine, and Diane says it's about Nora answering Krogstad's questions about Christine.

And what lines of dialogue does this event cover?

We think that it covers these lines:

KROGSTAD: I was sitting over at Olsen's Restaurant and I saw your husband going down the street-
NORA: Oh yes.
KROGSTAD: With a lady.
NORA: So?
KROGSTAD: I wonder if you'll allow me to ask if that lady was Mrs. Linde?
NORA: Yes.
KROGSTAD: Just arrived in town?
NORA: Yes, today.
KROGSTAD: She's a good friend of yours?
NORA: Yes, she is. But I can't see—
KROGSTAD: I also knew her at one time.
NORA: I'm aware of that.
KROGSTAD: Really? That's what I thought. Well then, let me get right to the point: Is Mrs. Linde getting a job at the bank?
NORA: Why do you think you can cross-examine me, Mr. Krogstad? You, who's just one of my husband's employees? But since, you ask, you might as well know: yes, Mrs. Linde

got a job. And I arranged it all for her, Mr. Krogstad. Now you know.

KROGSTAD: As I thought.

NORA: (*Pacing the floor.*) Oh, I should hope that one always has a little bit influence. Just because one is a woman, it doesn't follow that—when one is in an inferior position, Mr. Krogstad, one ought to be very careful with somebody who—

KROGSTAD: Who has influence?

NORA: Exactly.

That, we say is the dialogue that covers the third event.

But suddenly Diane voices an objection. When Nora goes on about Krogstad's "inferior position," that isn't about Mrs. Linde anymore. Maybe the event ends when Krogstad says, "As I thought."

When I imagine myself inside the circumstances, says Diane, which I am better able to do now because I have experienced them firsthand, I feel like a change happens at that point.

Then change where your third event ends, says the teacher. These beginnings and endings, these boundaries between events are open to adjustment. Do not carve them in stone. If your experience of the circumstances contradicts what you have marked, change your marks. These events are meant to serve as signposts to guide you. If they lead to a dead end, they are not achieving their purpose.

If the third event ends with Krogstad's "As I thought," then the fourth event begins with Nora's, "Oh, I should hope that one..."

That's right, says Diane. And you have said that a transition is often accompanied by a change of body posture or movement and Ibsen has indicated that right at this moment; Nora begins "*Pacing the floor.*"

Good point, says the teacher. So, what is this fourth event and where does it feel like it ends?

I have been quiet because I am having feelings of misgiving. I've done something like this before in other acting classes. It was called, marking "beats." But when I tried to get a clear understanding as to what a "beat" was, I could never quite grasp it. It seemed precise and yet vague at the same time. In the end, I hated marking up a script in this way because it seemed so dry and clinical

Then I learned to analyze a script in terms of objectives, obstacles and strategies. And it was useful, but still seemed so distant from the living, beating pulse of the material. When I worked with objectives and obstacles and strategies, I felt like I was standing outside the world of the play looking in through a window, when what I desperately wanted was to be inside.

Now, once again, I am marking up a script and it feels dry and lifeless. I hate it. But what am I to do? I'll just have to slog through.

So now we look through the script to find where the fourth event is and what we will call it.

Even though, Diane says slowly, they talk for a long time about Nora's influence on Torvald next, I don't think that we can call all of that talk one event. I would divide this whole section on "influence" like this:

NORA: (*Pacing the floor.*) Oh, I should hope that one always has a little bit of influence. Just because one is a woman, it doesn't follow that—when one is in an inferior position, Mr. Krogstad, one ought to be very careful with somebody who—
KROGSTAD: Who has influence?
NORA: Exactly.

I would call that an event in itself, says Diane. And I would call it "lording it over him." That's an important event for Nora because it's the first time she exercises any power over Krogstad. At least it *feels* like a separate event to me. It feels like I'm giving him a warning.

Even though, says the teacher, we are trying to identify the large events, I would agree with you on this one. But that brings up a question. Steven, does this feel like a separate event to you? And if so, what would you call it?

It does feel like a separate event to me and frankly it feels like she's putting me down, disrespecting me. I feel like I'm being put in my place, so I would call it, "getting kicked."

So what do your lists look like at this point?

Diane shows hers:

1) Play with the kids.
   Krogstad comes in and interrupts.
2) Find out what Krogstad wants.
3) Get Krogstad to leave by answering his questions.
4) Stand up to Krogstad.
5) Issue a warning to Krogstad by reminding him of his place.

Wait a minute, says the teacher. Your number four is one I haven't heard about. Where does "stand up to Krogstad" come in?

Well, confesses Diane, I did add one in. When Nora says "Why do you think you can cross-examine me Mr. Krogstad...?" I felt that it deserved some kind of recognition as an event. It feels like an important moment to me. I didn't bring it up earlier because I wanted to go along with Steven's ideas about the scene.

You've got to find these events from your character's point of view, admonishes the teacher. But the temptation to narrow these events down to each small change will give us so many that the list will become unwieldy. We are trying to mark the broad events not each individual change.

I don't mean to say that individual changes aren't important, they are. They are, in fact, crucial. But we will immobilize ourselves with details if we do this kind of analysis now. Keep what you have, but let's move on.

Steven, what is on your list?

I show mine:

1) Come in the door.
2) Get Nora to give me her attention.
3) Find out about Christine Linde.
4) Absorb a put-down about my place with respect to the Helmers.

OK, says the teacher. "Absorbing" is a verb, an action word, so I will accept it. What's the next event?

The next event Diane says, is about *using* the influence that Nora says she has.

I'm getting a headache. This feels like torture, I think to myself. We're in our heads and we'll never get out. But the teacher is speaking.

What lines of dialogue does this event cover?

This one is tough, but Diane says it covers the following lines:

KROGSTAD: (*Changing tone.*) Mrs. Helmer, would you be good enough to use your influence on my behalf?
NORA: What? What do you mean?
KROGSTAD: Would you be kind enough to make sure that I keep my inferior position at the bank?
NORA: What do you mean? Who's trying to take it away from you?
KROGSTAD: Oh, you don't have to play the innocent with me. I understand perfectly well that your friend doesn't want to run the risk of seeing me again; and now I also understand who to thank for being let go.

Now right here, says Diane, Krogstad has brought up a new fact to Nora. Nora begins to realize that Krogstad thinks that she got him fired. She didn't know that before, so is that a new event?

Since they return so quickly to the use of her influence, says the teacher, I would not mark it as a large event, but it is an important fact within this event. Keep going.

NORA: But I promise you—
KROGSTAD: Yes, yes, yes. But here's the point: there's still time, and I'd advise you to use your influence to prevent it.

That, we say, is the end of this event. Diane calls it "finding out why Krogstad needs my influence" and I call it "soliciting a favor by asking and threatening."

What's the next event? the teacher asks, but I notice that he looks less than pleased.

The next one, we say, covers the following dialogue and Diane calls it "denying any influence," and I call it "batting down her objections:"

NORA: But Mr. Krogstad, I have no influence at all.
KROGSTAD: No? I thought a minute ago you said—
NORA: I didn't mean it that way. What makes you think I've got any sort of influence over my husband in things like that?
KROGSTAD: Oh. I've known your husband since we were students together—and I don't think our Bank Manager has any more will power than any other married man.

What's the next event? asks the teacher.

Next, says Diane, is an event she calls, "standing up to Krogstad again" and I call, "absorbing threats from Nora." It covers the following dialogue:

NORA: You talk like that about my husband and I'll show you the door.
KROGSTAD: The lady has courage.
NORA: I'm not afraid of you any more. Soon after New Year's I'll be done with the whole business.

The teacher asks for our list of events so far. As usual, Diane goes first. She has amended some of her wording:

1) Play with the kids.
   Krogstad comes in and interrupts.
2) Find out what Krogstad wants.
3) Get Krogstad to leave by answering his questions.
4) Stand up to Krogstad by reminding him of his position.
5) Warn Krogstad of my power.
6) Find out why Krogstad wants my influence.
7) Deny any influence over my husband.
8) Stand up to Krogstad by threatening to throw him out of my house and by telling him he no longer scares me.

I'm barely hanging in, but I show my list of events so far:

1) Come in the door.
2) Get Nora to give me her attention.
3) Find out about Christine Linde.
4) Absorb a put-down about my place with respect to the Helmers.
5) Get a favor from Nora by asking directly and by threatening.
6) Bat down Nora's objections to helping me.
7) Absorb Nora's threat to throw me out.

This is good work, says the teacher, but you're only a page and a half into the scene. I'm afraid I've not explained myself very well. This is all too detailed for our immediate purposes.

I will divide the scene into large events myself so you can see more clearly what I'm getting at. Remember, we are trying to find the contour, the shape of the scene so that we can use it as a guide for an improvisation that will follow the scene as written by Ibsen more closely than we have before. Here are the larger divisions I would make, keeping in mind that Krogstad is the "leading" character:

1) Watching Nora playing a game with her children.
2) Interrupting the game.
3) Finding out about Christine Linde.
4) Asking for Nora's influence to help me keep my job.
5) Explaining what the job I will lose means to me.
6) Nora refuses to help. (This is a trigger for the next event.)
7) Forcing her to help.
8) Nora still refuses to help. (This is a trigger for the next event.)
9) Reminding her of the terms of our loan agreement.
10) Getting her to confess to the forgery.
11) Threatening to take her to court.
12) Leaving.

This is what I am getting at. Isn't this more what it feels like?

He's right. He didn't go through tortuous twists and convolutions to come up with that list. He saw clearly the large sections and just wrote them down. His list tells the story without following each tiny change. I think I could even do this.

List the large events that push the story forward, says the teacher. It will be much easier for you to live inside these larger circumstances and to remember them, than to focus on every turn of the scene.

Inside these larger events, of course, are a whole host of smaller events that will hopefully be triggered by looking at these bigger ones. If they are not, then we will find out in our next improvisation.

We can always get more detailed. But if those details fill themselves in without our intellectual interference, all the better. We only need to get down to the moment by moment level you have been creating if we need to. First, it is best to keep your list of events simple so that you can easily execute them without ransacking your memory for every twist and turn of the scene.

Oh, I think, praise this man. His words are like music.

So everything we just did is worthless? Diane asks.

Not at all, answers the teacher. It is not particularly *useful* at this point. Such a detailed list will only put your creative instincts in a straitjacket right now. I do not mean to imply that you do not need to know what you are doing every moment that you are on stage or in front of a camera. But right now you are still narrowing down, step by step, the circumstances of the scene.

Are you beginning to see that what we are doing here is getting closer and closer to the ultimate circumstances of the scene, which when reduced to their most microscopic level are the lines themselves and what's between them?

Is it coming clear that by the time we get to the lines, they'll arise naturally from the circumstances and from our emotional connection to those circumstances?

We began with a core circumstance, then added in one or two other important circumstances and now we are making a list of more circumstances in the order they occur in the written scene. In other words, first this event happens, then this one and so on. We are closing in on the scene.

But this list is a rather radical departure from what we have been doing so far and there is a great danger in it. We might feel the pressure to put most of our attention on the correct order and less on playing as ourselves and on the effect that the other actor has on us.

We must fight this possible dehumanizing effect by telling ourselves that we are still exploring. We must not let it keep us from discovering our own responses and the unique behavior that will bring non-clichéd life to the material. We are still going to play inside these circumstances, search out possibilities, find the *feeling* life of the material.

I'll show you, says the teacher, what I mean.

WORKING AT HOME

At home, go over the material and make a list of the major sections of the scene. These "events" should be based on where you *feel* these changes are.

This step is fraught with danger. Because it depends to some extent on an intellectual procedure, this list can become dry and disconnected from the feeling life of the actor. That is why it is so critical that the actor has first *experienced* some of the core circumstances. The list should be feeling-based, meaning that you should *feel t*hat there is a major event here which *feels* like it changes to a different major event there...and so on. You are going to use this list for improvisations, so shortness is a value. But too short a list will give you nothing to play and nowhere to go. Make it short enough to be interesting and long enough to cover the subject.

This list is to help you work on the material in smaller sections. We use the largest divisions because they are more manageable, but also in the hopes that they will trigger the details contained within them. When a section is not understood, we can move in more microscopically and examine it in detail. Ultimately, when performing the part on stage or in front of the camera, we may need only to remind ourselves of the first one or two larger events to set our wills and emotions in action.

It is important to remember that breaking a script down into beats, finding objectives, obstacles to those objectives, and strategies for overcoming those obstacles are useful tools but can be mere intellectual constructs that disengage the actor from his instincts.

Stanislavski meant this kind of analysis to do the opposite. It is meant to free the actor's instincts, excite his will and lure his emotions. It is important for actors to understand that playing an objective is not the same thing as acting. It is a tool that helps us act. It points us in the direction we want to go but it doesn't take us there.

Many scenes are ruined because an actor plays only the objective and misses the natural ups and downs of the scene as it unfolds. Working out all these objectives, obstacles, and strategies give us information about the scene but we must keep in mind that the information about acting, is not acting itself.

A useful objective is one that pulls the character towards the future. It must always be ahead of him and it must be something that he truly desires. For this reason, it is a good idea to think of an objective this way: *What is the object of my desire?*

It is not enough to say I want my daughter's love. It is too general. I cannot see it or taste it or touch it. It does not excite my will toward it. But if I say the object of my desire is for my daughter to rest her head on my chest like she did when she was seven, then I can see it and feel it. My will yearns for it, and when the will yearns, the emotions follow.

The "event" breakdown we are doing is an attempt to divide the work into manageable sections without damaging the emotional power of the material.

PROCESS REVIEW

14. **Make a list of the major events in the scene.** Give each one of these events a name, a name that is characterized by an active verb. In other words, these events should be phrased as actions. Keep this list as short as possible while still covering the whole scene. Too much detail at this point will only overwhelm and paralyze your creative imagination. This list should be based on your *feeling* of where the larger events are, based on your improvisations. Dry analysis will appeal only to the intellect and will not excite the will or engage the emotions.

CHAPTER 8

Speaking Your Heart

You are now going to tell each other how you *feel* about the events from your list.

This is all the teacher says.

He is looking at us, and we are looking at each other. I volunteer to be the guinea pig and turn toward Diane with the events list in my lap. To refresh my memory I look down to see if I am following them correctly. The first one is "watching her play with her kids." I launch right in:

I feel a little uneasy because I have opened the door without anyone's permission even though I did knock. As I realize that you are playing with your children, I feel a wave of guilt rush through me for intruding.

Then I resent the carefree fun you are having knowing that I might have been home playing with *my* kids if your husband hadn't just fired me. I feel a little vengeful as well because I suspect that you and my old lover schemed to have me thrown out.

I push down some of my feelings because I am here to ask you a favor, because you are the boss's wife and because I'm not sure that you have done what I think you have. I'm not even entirely certain that the woman I saw you with earlier was, in fact, Christine Linde. I haven't seen her for tears, I mean *years*.

That slip of the tongue is very useful, interrupts the teacher, but go on.

I know why the word "tears" slipped out, I say to myself. I shed a lot of tears over Christine's cruel rejection of me, and the pain is still not very far away.

I look down at my list to see what the next event is. It is the interruption itself.

After watching you for a few moments, I settle myself enough to be civil and try to get your attention. When I do, you don't seem very happy to see me and want to know what I am doing here, assuming that I want to see your husband. When I tell you I want to talk to you, you send the children out. At least, I feel, you are taking me seriously by doing that. I do, however, hear one child wonder if the "strange" man will hurt you. That feels like another kick in the stomach.

When you give me your attention I reassure you that I am not here to collect a loan payment from you, but that my business is very serious indeed, and to make you understand that you had better listen to what I have to say, I warn you that the cheeriness of your holiday celebrations are at stake.

After that, you seem to have some time for me. I am feeling quite resentful and bitter that I have to threaten you before I can be granted an "audience" with you. But now I can get down to business.

I look down at the list before I go on. I realize that I am adding in all kinds of details, but the teacher hasn't stopped me. Maybe I'm doing something right, so I continue.

I tell you that I saw Torvald walking with a woman just a few minutes ago and ask if the woman was Christine Linde. I don't feel hostile at this moment, I honestly just want an answer to the question. When you confirm that it was her, something in me sinks. My suspicions are starting to come true. I wonder what she is doing here and I feel my breathing change. I feel strangely vulnerable and it makes me uncomfortable.

I need to know now if my suspicions are true. The emotions I am feeling make me want to hide them from you, so I ask innocently if you are good friends with Mrs. Linde and when you say that you are, I innocently tell you that I too knew her once.

But this question has me quivering. There is a trap in it for you. I am really trying to find out if the two of you talked about our old love relationship behind my back. A lot is riding on your answer, and when you say that you were aware that we knew each other, my worst fears are confirmed and I get to the main point. I want to know if Christine has gotten a job at the bank.

Instead of answering me, however, you suddenly attack me. You hurt me by reminding me of my menial position and I want to hurt you back for it.

Then you have the nerve to tell me that you were the one who made it possible for Christine to get my job and all my suspicions are confirmed. I am still smarting from your put-down and from the way I have been pushed out of my position at the bank, when you remind me *again* of what a peon I am.

OK, I think to myself, that's how you want to play? Well I have a few weapons of my own. But before I unleash them on you, I ask if you'll use your *powerful* influence to help me. At this point, of course, I fully expect you to refuse me. You make me repeat my request and you play dumb. You pathetically act innocent when I tell you that I know what's been going on with you, Christine and Torvald. It makes me sick.

Then you have the nerve to threaten to throw me out because I insult Torvald. You don't seem to be taking me very seriously and *I* am insulted by that, so I make it clear to you that I will fight to the death for that job.

Then I can feel your contempt. I know what you think of me. What everyone in this town thinks of me. Nils Krogstad, a dirty little money grubber who will fight to the death for every coin he can get his greedy hands on.

Well, I'm not who you think I am. I feel a desperate need to be understood *correctly*; to be seen for who I really am. It goes deeper than money with me. I want *respect* and a future for my children, that's why I will fight for this job. For years no one would invite me or my children into their homes, people wouldn't look me in the eyes when I passed them on the street, no one would employ me and I was forced into the loan business. I have a right to live too, you know. But you and your husband are trying to destroy me and I won't let that happen.

And after I explain all this to you, you still refuse to help me. I can't believe it. You so look down on me that even after I explain myself you *still* won't give me a hand up.

I knew people were low, but this truly embitters me, so I do the thing I have been hoping I would not have to do. I tell you I can force you to help me. I know I have the forged loan document on me and now I also know that I will use it against you. You think of me as a disgusting little weasel, well that's exactly what I'll be. I did you a favor years ago, a favor that saved your husband's life and now you won't lift a finger to help me. Well, screw you.

But you surprise me. You give me an idea I hadn't really thought of. You are worried that I will the tell Torvald of the existence of the loan. I realize that he doesn't know about it, but I haven't understood just what his ignorance of it means to you. You become very upset at the thought that he will find out about this loan and so I hint that I might tell him about it. Unfortunately this threat, although it upsets you greatly, is not enough to get you to help me. So I move on to my biggest weapon.

I ask if all you're worried about is some domestic trouble with your husband and you feign ignorance. You wonder what I mean. All right, I think to myself, if you want to play dumb, then I'll walk you step by step to your enlightenment.

You want to make it hard for me, then I'll make it hard for you. I'll treat you like a hostile witness. I am a lawyer after all.

I make you go over the terms and circumstances of the loan by asking you leading questions. I enjoy watching you get closer and closer to my trap. Finally, we get to the subject of your father's death. I pretend to be genuinely puzzled by it. I gently point out to you that your father affixed his signature to the loan document three days after he died. I wonder if you can explain that to me. Your silence is so satisfying. Don't have a word to say, do you? This is delicious. You're suddenly in a trap you can't get out of and you don't even know how you got there; never saw it coming I, mister "inferior," am now your superior. It takes just another question or two before you are confessing to the forgery.

But you surprise me again. My satisfaction is short-lived. You don't seem to realize what the consequences of your crime are. You justify it by saying that you *had* to do it.

What infuriates me is that you thought of what was good for your husband and for your father but didn't spend a drop of your concern for me. You gave me a fraudulent document. If you hadn't been able to pay off the money, I would have gone to your father or his estate for the money that was owed me. But I would not have had the right because he *never really signed the loan guarantee*. Where do you think I got the money to loan to you? Don't you think *I* have people *I* have to pay back?

You put me in a very dangerous situation, and you don't seem to care. You tell me that you weren't thinking about me, that you couldn't stand me. Well, the truth is out. You have hated me from the first day you came to me. You've loved my money but despised me. Just like everyone else. Well, I want to hurt you back, make you pay. When I get bitten, I bite back one hundred times harder.

I tell you that you will be judged by a court of law that doesn't care *why* you did what you did only that you did it. And when you insult me again, calling me an incompetent lawyer, I warn you for a final time. I tell you that if you don't use your influence on your husband to get me my job back, I'll take you down. And then I leave.

Diane's eyes are locked on me and I am breathing hard. I didn't realize I had so much to say. I didn't use just the list of events, I had the scene on my lap as well and often looked at it. I wasn't sure if this was OK but the teacher didn't snatch it away, as he sometimes does, so I continued to use it.

How do you feel? asks the teacher.

Good, I say.

You should. You did a wonderful job. The list of events gives us the major sequence of actions as they occur in the script. But it does *not* show us how one event becomes the next and that linkage is all-important. What you do by telling your partner how you feet about the external events is to create an *inner* line of action. Stanislavski puts it this way: "Now the process goes deeper, it goes down from the realm of the external...into that of the inner, spiritual life. And this is brought about with the help of the actor's creative emotions.

"To do this he must set himself at the very center...he must be there in person, not seeing himself as an observer.... This moment is what we in actor's jargon call the state of 'I am,' it is the point where I begin to feel myself in the thick of things, where I begin to coalesce with all the circumstances suggested by the playwright and by the actor, begin to have the right to be part of them. This right is not achieved immediately, it is achieved gradually."[1]

What you just accomplished is the result of the work you did before. You were only able to do what you did because you had experienced the basic circumstances of Ibsen's scene first. The feelings you described and felt were not preconceived ideas, they were not mere concepts in your head, they came from walking the character's circumstances in your own shoes. The analysis you did after each improvisation also helped give you the feeling of living inside Krogstad's world. You understand it not just with your head, but with your heart, not just in your mind, but in your body.

These two lines, the external and the internal, weave together to give you that feeling of "I am."

Now, says the teacher, it is Diane's turn.

Diane takes a deep breath and turns towards me.

I am playing with my children, she begins, because I am in a great mood. Not only have I gotten my friend a job at my

---

[1]Stanislavski, Constantine, *Creating A Role*, trans., E.R Hapgood, Routledge Press, NYC, 1989, pp. 25–26.

husband's bank, not only is money finally *not* going to be so scarce, not only is it Christmas time, and not only will I soon pay off my loan to Krogstad, but I have just learned that he is now an employee of my husband's. I don't have to bow and scrape to him anymore. I don't have to fear him. Things just couldn't be much better. All of my concerns and worries have washed off me and I just feel like shouting, "To hell with everything!"

I am feeling very playful and suggest a game of hide-and-seek with my kids. I am going to hide first. The children are laughing and shouting and I am too. None of us are taking this game too seriously. I feel completely safe and secure. In fact, I have never felt better in my entire life.

Suddenly I hear a strange male voice and it startles and scares me viscerally. I am shocked and then annoyed when I see that the voice belongs to Krogstad. I immediately wonder where my husband is. If he sees me talking with Krogstad he'll ask me questions I don't want to answer. What is this man doing here on Christmas eve? How dare you come into my house, scare the stuffing out of me and interrupt my time with my kids? All I want to do is get rid of him.

When you tell me you are here to talk to me and not to my husband, I am puzzled and concerned and send the children out of the room. Even they, after seeing you so briefly, can sense that you're a strange man. I would rather have this conversation somewhere else, but if I go out on the street with Krogstad, Torvald might see us. But if I have a long conversation with him here, Torvald might well walk in on that. Oh, I hate this.

To get rid of you quickly, I tell you that I won't have your money until the first of the year and then you actually threaten me. What a dirty weasel you are! That threat gets my attention and I ask you to get to the point. I need you to do all of this quickly because I have no idea when Torvald is coming back. I feel very put out about all this but agree to give you a moment.

Then you start to ask questions about Christine Linde. I don't get this. What does she have to do with anything? This seems like a dangerous waste of time to me. I give you short answers until I get fed up with the whole thing. I am annoyed at this intrusion for what I feel is a trivial discussion and I tell you so.

Frankly, I enjoy putting you in your place. I have been afraid of you for years and now I don't have to be. I let you know that I have a little bit of power too.

But then you ask a surprising thing. You want to know if I.will use my bit of power to help you. What on earth for, I wonder. I can't fathom what help I can be to you. You ask me if I will help you keep your job at the bank and I am truly puzzled. I have no idea what you are talking about. And then you insult me.

This mean man, I think to myself, who got me a loan only on the coldest of conditions, who has been making me pay for years, who is standing in *my* house, accuses me of playing some kind of game and *then* says that I'm the one responsible for him losing his job. I'm beginning to wonder about the man's sanity.

I have to tell you that I don't have the kind of power you think I do. I feel a little guilty now for bragging about getting Christine a job at the bank. I see how serious you are and I tell you in no uncertain terms that I simply don't have the kind of influence over my husband that you think I do.

I'm scared to death to bring your name up to Torvald. He has no idea that I even know you. It will make him extremely suspicious if I plead your case to him.

But you next insult Torvald by saying that he is just as weak as any other married man, meaning that I could hen-peck him into doing whatever I want him to and that is just too much for me. I don't have to stand here in my own house and listen to insults hurled at my husband. I am infuriated. Just who do you think you are? I tell you I'm not afraid of you anymore because soon you'll be paid off.

But then I get another surprise. As you tell me why your menial job at my husband's bank means so much to you, I start to feel sympathy for your predicament. I don't want to, but I do. I see that it isn't just money with you but the recovery of your pride and the respect of your children.

I'm not exactly won over, but I have softened toward you. But no matter what I feel, I have to tell you the sad truth; that I am powerless to help you.

Now you get truly nasty. My stomach falls out when you threaten to force me to help you. My mind immediately runs to my greatest fear: That Torvald will find out about what I did. And from a stranger, a hostile stranger at that.

What I did for Torvald was noble and good but if he finds it out from you it will only seem sordid, devious and disobedient. I can't believe anyone would stoop so low. But my pleas fall on deaf ears and I pull myself together when I realize that your telling Torvald will only make him hate you more. At this moment I despise you for threatening to reveal my secret.

Then I get scared because you don't stop. I become very wary when you start asking questions about the terms of our loan agreement. I don't understand where all this is going but I feel great danger nearby. I feel like I'm being led to slaughter but I cannot see from what direction the blow will come. This whole series of questions makes me uneasy. The sense of danger increases when you ask about the date of my father's death. I feel like my face is flushing and that you can read the fear on my face. You are so close to a secret that I thought was completely safe from discovery. I hate you for sniffing this out. You disgust me.

Since you have trapped me and uncovered what I thought was so well hidden, I simply confess. I will not give you the satisfaction of seeing my pain. But I am scared. I said I wasn't scared of you but right now I'm more scared than at any time since Torvald was sick. I feel contempt for you too. These feelings make me want to put a brave face on it all even though I'm afraid I'm going to burst out crying. Just a few minutes ago everything was going so well. I felt on top of the world. Now suddenly I feel at the bottom.

I pretend that this discovery of yours is of no consequence

anyway since the loan will be paid off soon, but you keep asking questions.

Finally I burst and tell you what I think of you and your loan. I tell you that the law will not punish me for helping my husband and keeping my father from further pain, but you shake my confidence when you say that the law doesn't take motives into account. I feel my whole body vibrating as you threaten me one final time and leave. I am stunned. I feel like my world has been shattered, like I cannot find solid ground to stand on. I am in shock.

Diane's voice is actually quivering. She has done all this mostly looking at me and sometimes looking down at the list of events and at the scene itself.

Good, says the teacher. You both have now tested the facts of the scene through your own personal emotions so that the life, the inner and outer circumstances of your roles, no longer feels alien. You are beginning to convey the living spirit that like a subterranean river flows under the external facts. You are finding the inner pattern of the life of a human being.[2]

Without forcing, and without giving the material a chance to intimidate you, you have found your way deeply into the way the characters think and feel. And you have not lost yourselves in the process. When you play a character you are not playing yourself, but you are *using* yourself.

This step in the process creates a pattern of inner action that connects and motivates the external events of the scene. As you see, these two planes, the outer and the inner, must be inextricably woven together. You just did some of this weaving. From here on in the weave will become deeper and richer.

Keep in mind, that the inner life you just created is in no way fixed. Tomorrow you may feel new and different responses to the circumstances and to your partner. That is good. You *want* to open up choices and explore possibilities before you make decisions.

---

2. Stanislavski, Constantine, *Creating A Role*, trans. E.R. Hapgood, Routledge Press, NYC, 1989, pp. 41–42.

But remember that the inner life you just verbalized was not arbitrary or preconceived. It was based on your understanding of the circumstances and their consistent logic. You injected *your* emotional life into *Ibsen's* circumstances and found an inner life for the characters.

So, I wonder to myself, maybe there is such a thing as "character" after all, a character called Steven/Krogstad. Maybe after some more exploration it might even be called Krogstad/Steven.

WORKING AT HOME

After creating the events list, read the scene again. If you want to amend your list, do so. It is meant to be an evolving document.

With the events list in your lap as well as the scene itself, express how you feel about each event. If details of the scene come up, let them. That is partly what the list is for; to trigger details. You do not need the other actor present.

The feelings you express should be based on the improvisational experiences you have had but can extend beyond them. If you have more than one feeling about an event express them all. This is not necessarily how you will play the part, it is meant to create an inner pattern, a river of feeling that connects one event to the next. The next day, you may feel differently about certain events or about the entire scene. And that is how it should be.

Part of the danger of the list is that the events look separate. It can be difficult to remember that they are connected. This exercise shows you the emotional logic of how one event leads to another.

When working on a part, this exercise is one you can do at many points in the process. If you find yourself saying "and then all of a sudden," or "for some reason," stop. It means that a piece of the emotional logic is missing. Mark that place in your script to work on later or search for that missing piece right away. But find it.

By bringing your feeling life to the characters' circumstances, you create an inner emotional pattern that follows and also creates the external events.

Please be careful here. One can misuse this exercise by fixing an emotional pattern in your mind. This exercise is not the same as scoring a role. You are not creating the emotional life of the character, memorizing it and bringing it to each performance. This would petrify the part. You must remember when you act with others to let them affect you. This exercise is meant to help you know what feelings connect the events together. The emotions may change moment to moment, hour to hour, day to day, rehearsal to rehearsal, performance to performance.

This does bring up a perplexing issue. If an actor plays only the emotions and actions he has created in his mind, he will be acting by himself. We have often seen student and professional actors act up a storm on stage to absolutely no effect because they ignored interacting with their fellow players. But if an actor believes that his performance depends only on his interaction with his scene partner, then what does he do if the actor gives him nothing, or if at an audition the casting director reads the other part with little or no expression? An actor must certainly allow himself to be affected by others, but on the other hand, he must not allow them to dictate his performance. It is a delicate balance.

What do you do, by the way, if you get little or nothing from an auditioner or actor? You play the meaning of the circumstances and the meaning of the words. If a casting director says in a flat, inexpressive voice, "I am responsible for the death your father," you play what is said, not how it is said. You cannot afford to abandon your responsibilities as an actor because someone else is doing his or her job poorly.

PROCESS REVIEW

15. **Tell your partner how you feel about the events.** This can also be done alone. Have the list of events where you can see it, but only refer to it when you have to. Then in your own words explain the events of the scene and the pattern of your inner life as you react to those events. Assume that you know and have experienced the basic circumstances of the play up to the point where your scene begins.

    This step creates the inner *feeling* line that gives life to the external events. Knowing the circumstances and then experiencing them with your own emotions prepares the way for this step. This step also helps to make clear how one event moves on to become another one, it shows the actor how the circumstances are connected.

CHAPTER 9

Playing Events

In this next exploration, or improvisation, you will try to play the events from your list in the same order they occur. You are still playing as yourselves, but now you can assume that you know as much about the circumstances as the characters do. You are not trying to play Krogstad and Nora, but the truth is that so much of your inner life has connected with theirs that you are already blended. It is time to think of yourselves as Steven/Krogstad and Diane/Nora.

There is one other difference in this improvisation. This time you may use any phrases or words of Ibsen's that you *feel the need of*, or love.

Be especially sensitive to following any actions that spring from feelings. Don't force or deliberately try to recreate any emotions, just let them come.

Don't worry if you do something that you think would be "inappropriate" to the character or the scene. That will only stifle your instincts. You are free to violate what you think are the boundaries of the text. We're not here to respect Ibsen, we're here to love him. After all, the characters don't know they're in an Ibsen play.

Diane jumps into the acting space and I position myself behind a door. I have the list of events in my hand and Diane has put hers nearby. This time we are in Ibsen's circumstances, not our own, and I am a weird combination of nervous and excited. I try to focus on why I am here at the Helmer house.

I remember that I was here earlier to see if my job was truly in jeopardy only to have my worst fears confirmed. I remember that my old lover Christine Linde is suddenly back in town and that I have seen her today both with Nora and Torvald Helmer.

But I remember something the teacher once told us. Before an exploration or a scene, think more about the future than the past. So I turn my mind to what is ahead of me, not what is behind.

I start to feel angry when I give rein to my suspicions that Nora and Christine plotted to have me removed but also remember to be polite with my boss's wife and that I am here to ask her a favor. I am also here to find out if Christine Linde is back in town. I don't particularly look forward to this conversation but I knock on the door.

When there is no answer, I knock again. I can't help noticing that the door is part way open and after there is no response to my second knock, I come in.

I heard laughter and shouting from outside the door and now I see the reason for it. The Helmer kids are playing. I feel a little embarrassed to be here on Christmas eve, but as usual, I have been forced to be the "bad guy." I lean in a bit, start to talk, but stop. I just feel so rude.

(After a moment, when there is some quiet, I speak.)

STEVEN/KROGSTAD: Uh, excuse me.

(Diane continues playing and doesn't answer. I try again, a little louder.)

STEVEN/KROGSTAD: Mrs. Helmer?

(Still no response from Diane. I am getting annoyed.)

STEVEN/KROGSTAD: Excuse me, Mrs. Helmer...?

(Diane gasps and pops up, her hand to her chest.)

DIANE/NORA: My god, you scared the hell out of me.

(She catches her breath and stares at me. She speaks in a low voice, staying right where she is.)

DIANE/NORA: What are you doing here?

(I stay by the doorway.)

STEVEN/KROGSTAD: I need to talk to you.

(Diane is staring hard at me.)

DIANE/NORA: My husband isn't here, Mr. Krogstad.

STEVEN/KROGSTAD: I realize that. I'm not here to see him, I'm here to see you.

(Diane looks around as if trying to gather her thoughts and sees the children. I am amazed to feel that there is real tension in the room. She bends down to speak to them. Her tone of voice is sweet and devoid of alarm.)

DIANE/NORA: Kids, I have to talk to a grown-up for a few minutes which will be very boring for you and probably for me, so why don't you go in to the other room and tell Anne-Marie to give you each a candy cane. Go on, scoot.

(She watches them go, then hurries to the door where I am still standing. There is panic in her voice.)

DIANE/NORA: What are you doing here?

(She looks quickly past me out the door.)

DIANE/NORA: You shouldn't be here. Look, I won't have the payment until the first of the month. I'll bring it to you at our usual place. Please, you should go now.

STEVEN/KROGSTAD: I'm sorry Mrs. Helmer, but I have to talk to you and it has to be now.

DIANE/NORA: Mr. Krogstad, what is this? It's Christmas eve.

STEVEN/KROGSTAD: I know that. And it'll be up to you how much Christmas cheer you have this holiday.

(This stops her cold. She looks at me a long moment, motions me into the room and shuts the door.)

DIANE/NORA: What is it Mr. Krogstad?

(I kind of like that I have flustered her and feel like dragging it out. I walk slowly past her and look around the room. At my leisure, I speak.)

STEVEN/KROGSTAD: I saw your husband and a woman walking down the street.

(That's all I say, knowing it will exasperate her. I feel like torturing her a little. She is still by the door but has turned to watch me.)

DIANE/NORA: Yes?

STEVEN/KROGSTAD: Well, I was wondering...

(And here I sit down. I wasn't invited to, but I didn't like the way she tried to get rid of me so quickly at the door, so I feel like settling in. And the thought occurs to me that I did this also in one of the early improvisations.)

STEVEN/KROGSTAD: ...if the woman was a, Mrs. Linde?

(Diane took a deep breath when I sat down. Unruffling her ruffled feathers I suppose. Her tone is very put upon.)

DIANE/NORA: Yes it was.

(I thought it was, but having it confirmed makes me uneasy.)

STEVEN/KROGSTAD: I see.

(I lean forward.)

STEVEN/KROGSTAD: When did she arrive in town?

DIANE/NORA: Today, as a matter of fact.

(I nod my head and stand up. My suspicions are quickly turning into realities. For some reason I have picked up from the table an elegant porcelain figurine of a woman. I start to circle the table. I say the next line looking at the figurine.)

STEVEN/KROGSTAD: And...are you good friends with her?

(Diane is watching me with the figurine, obviously annoyed that I have picked it up so familiarly.)

DIANE/NORA: look, I don't know where you get off giving me the third degree...

(I look up at her.)

STEVEN/KROGSTAD: I also knew her once upon a time.

DIANE/NORA: I'm aware of that.

STEVEN/KROGSTAD: Oh, really?

(I put the figurine down and walk over to her.)

STEVEN/KROGSTAD: Let me get to the point. Is Christine Linde getting a job at the bank?

DIANE/NORA: I don't see what business that is of yours. I don't have to answer any of your questions, Mr. Krogstad, if I don't want to.

(Diane moves from the door and crosses to the table. As she speaks, she picks up the figurine and puts it up on a mantle, away from me.)

DIANE/NORA: You should remember that you are talking to your boss's wife and show a little more respect. But I will tell you that, yes, my friend *is* getting a job at my husband's bank and *I* helped her to get it.

(She is leaning against the wall, seeming very self-satisfied.)

STEVEN/KROGSTAD: I see.

DIANE/NORA: Yes. Just because I'm a woman, Mr. Krogstad, doesn't mean that I don't have a little power of my own.

(Diane has crossed her arms and legs.)

STEVEN/KROGSTAD: Yes, I realize that.

DIANE/NORA: So if you're quite finished, you can see yourself out.

(Diane picks up a small container with macaroons it.)

STEVEN/KROGSTAD: But I'm afraid I'm *not* finished Mrs. Helmer.

(Her treatment of me is really making me angry. Diane is silent as I move away from the door and toward her. I speak to her in a controlled voice.)

STEVEN/KROGSTAD: What I am wondering, Mrs. Helmer, is if you will use some of your power on my behalf?

(Diane is standing straight up now, tension in her body.)

DIANE/NORA: What do you mean?

(Good. She seems a little less self-satisfied now.)

STEVEN/KROGSTAD: I want to know if you will help me keep my little job at, as you call it, your "husband's" bank?

DIANE/NORA: But you already have a job at the bank. Dr. Rank told me that.

STEVEN/KROGSTAD: Don't play stupid with me. Do I look

like an idiot? I know you and Christine talked your husband into firing me and giving my job to Christine. I know that. What I want to know is, will you talk him into changing his mind?

DIANE/NORA: Mr. Krogstad, what you just said didn't happen. Mrs. Linde and I did not...

STEVEN/KROGSTAD: Say whatever you want. I know what I know. Will you use your influence to help me or won't you?

DIANE/NORA: But I don't have the kind of influence you think I do.

STEVEN/KROGSTAD: But you just told me you do.

DIANE/NORA: I...I shouldn't have said that.

(She sets the macaroon container down.)

STEVEN/KROGSTAD: No, not in front of me. For *me* you have no power but for your *friends*, you have plenty.

DIANE/NORA: Mr. Krogstad, please...

(I put up my hand to stop her.)

STEVEN/KROGSTAD: I'm not playing games, Mrs. Helmer. This job means everything to me and I'm going to fight for it.

DIANE/NORA: I can see that.

(Diane says this with such disdain that I want to hit her. I compose myself quickly and move away from her.)

STEVEN/KROGSTAD: Let me explain something to you.

(I can't look at her because this is hard for me to say. I feel embarrassed.)

STEVEN/KROGSTAD: I'm sure you know, just as everyone in this whole damn town seems to know, that some years ago I got into a little legal trouble. And even though my case never went to trial, everyone here turned their backs on me like I was a leper, or some kind of infectious disease.

(I turn right toward her and my words come spilling out.)

STEVEN/KROGSTAD: There was no guilty verdict from a court, but that didn't stop people from condemning me anyway. Nobody would hire me, my reputation was ruined and I had nowhere to go. Now I had two kids to raise. Their mother is dead. How was I supposed to live? Even I have a right to do that, don't I? All that was open to me was this loan business you are so familiar with.

(Diane moves away from the wall and sits down, not looking at me. For some reason, this slows me down a little.)

STEVEN/KROGSTAD: Finally, after years, I got a measly little job at the bank. But at least, it was a real job. One my kids could respect. It was my first step back to a good name. I haven't gone *near* my old work. And now your husband wants to destroy it all. Everything I've worked for. Wants to force me back into the mud. But I have to keep that from happening.

DIANE/NORA: I am truly sorry for you, Mr. Krogstad. You have had a very hard time, I can see that, and I feel terrible for you. But my husband must have his reasons for letting you go and I can't interfere in his business.

(Diane stands up and walks to the door.)

DIANE/NORA: You have mistaken the extent of my influence over him, I'm afraid. Unfortunately, I can't offer you any help.

(She puts her hand on the doorknob.)

STEVEN/KROGSTAD: Can't offer, or won't offer?

DIANE/NORA: Mr. Krogstad...

STEVEN/KROGSTAD: I can make you help me, if I want to, you understand?

(Diane takes her hand off the doorknob and looks at me.)

DIANE/NORA: Meaning?

STEVEN/KROGSTAD: Meaning I can force you.

(Diane takes a step towards me.)

DIANE/NORA: You wouldn't tell my husband about the loan?

(She looks a little shaky and I'm glad. This seems to be a vulnerable spot. I turn my back on her and move toward Torvald's office, open the door and look in. This is where, just twenty short minutes ago, he informed me of my impending dismissal.)

STEVEN/KROGSTAD: *(Still looking into Torvald's office.)* And what if I did?

DIANE/NORA: Please, Mr. Krogstad. That would...*(She takes several breaths.)* that would be such a...a betrayal. When he finds out what I did for him, I want it to come from me. It means so much to me, please...you know it would be wrong of you to do.

(I turn back and look at her. I just leave her hanging there. I am completely unmoved by this plea. When I asked for her help she refused me. Why shouldn't I do the same. I lean against the wall and cross my legs. Diane starts to shake her head.)

DIANE/NORA: I don't understand people like you. How do you sleep at night? How can you do this to people?

STEVEN/KROGSTAD: Don't fool yourself, Mrs. Helmer. You'd do the same thing in my position. The truth is, you don't know who you are until your back is forced to the wall. A person does what he has to.

DIANE/NORA: Well then you go right ahead and do what you have to do, Mr. Krogstad...

(Diane comes into the room and starts picking the children's clothing off the floor. She folds them and sets them on the table.)

DIANE/NORA: ...because it doesn't matter. You go right ahead. My husband will see you for what you really are and you'll have no chance of ever getting your job back.

(She is back over by the door now. My left hand feels for the forged loan document concealed inside the breast pocket of my coat. It's still there.)

STEVEN/KROGSTAD: You still don't get it, do you?

DIANE/NORA: Oh, I understand you perfectly.

STEVEN/KROGSTAD: I don't think you do. I think I need to remind you of a few things Mrs. Helmer.

(Diane is staring at me. Concern on her face.)

STEVEN/KROGSTAD: When your husband was sick, you came to me for a great deal of money.

DIANE/NORA: And?

STEVEN/KROGSTAD: And, I got it for you, didn't I?

DIANE/NORA: And I've been paying you back. Every month.

STEVEN/KROGSTAD: I said I'd get you that money if you signed a contract with me, isn't that correct?

DIANE/NORA: Yes, and I signed it.

STEVEN/KROGSTAD: You did. And I also told you that I needed someone to guarantee the loan. That if you couldn't pay me back, that I needed a guarantee that someone else would.

DIANE/NORA: Yes, yes. My father. He guaranteed the loan.

STEVEN/KROGSTAD: Yes he did. And after I got the loan document back from you, properly executed, I got you the money.

DIANE/NORA: If you're trying to make out that you did me a favor, Mr. Krogstad, it just isn't so. It was a business affair, and I have held up my part of it.

STEVEN/KROGSTAD: Have you, really? Well let me just ask you this? Your father was very sick at the time, was he not?

DIANE/NORA: He was quite sick, yes.

STEVEN/KROGSTAD: He was dying, wasn't he?

DIANE/NORA: Yes.

STEVEN/KROGSTAD: Do you remember the date of his death?

DIANE/NORA: Yes, of course. He died on September 29th.

STEVEN/KROGSTAD: September 29th, that's right.

(I reach into my coat, take out a document, not the loan paper, and brandish it.)

STEVEN/KROGSTAD: I looked it up.

(I put the paper back in my pocket and wander over to the table. I pick up the macaroon container.)

STEVEN/KROGSTAD: And that brings us to a strange thing, Mrs. Helmer.

DIANE/NORA: And that would be?

STEVEN/KROGSTAD: The strange thing is, Mrs. Helmer, the thing I just can't figure out…

(I reach into my jacket pocket and take out the loan document.)

STEVEN/KROGSTAD: …is that your father signed this document three days after he died. Can you explain that to me, Mrs. Helmer?

(I have put the paper back and opened the container. I take

a bite of a macaroon. Diane looks like a deer caught in the headlights,)

STEVEN/KROGSTAD: How someone can sign a document after he's dead? I can't figure that out.

(Diane says nothing.)

STEVEN/KROGSTAD: And the other interesting thing is that the handwriting of the date, supposedly written by your father, is in a handwriting I recognize. Somebody, and I think we both know who, filled in the date for your father.

(I take another bite, take a handkerchief from my coat pocket, and wipe my mouth.

STEVEN/KROGSTAD: Now the only question left is this: whether the signature of your father on the document is genuine.

(Diane is leaning against the door with her hands behind her. Her head is down and she is quiet.)

STEVEN/KROGSTAD: It is his signature on this paper isn't it?

(I walk toward her.)

STEVEN/KROGSTAD: Mrs. Helmer, It is your father's signature, isn't it?

(Diane answers in a very quiet voice, not looking at me, but before she speaks, she lifts her head and shakes it.)

DIANE/NORA: No.

STEVEN/KROGSTAD: No?

DIANE/NORA: I signed his name.

STEVEN/KROGSTAD: Do you realize what you're saying? Do you understand you've committed a crime, broken the law?

(Diane bolts from the door.)

DIANE/NORA: What else could I do? My husband was *dying*.

(Diane turns towards me. I remain near the door.)

DIANE/NORA: Do you understand? Dying!

(She looks around the room thinking that she might have been loud enough for the children to hear. She lowers her voice.)

DIANE/NORA: You said a person does what they have to do. Well, that's what I did!

(I find myself speaking calmly.)

STEVEN/KROGSTAD: But why not just have your father sign the paper? I don't get it. Why risk being found out?

DIANE/NORA: My father was dying. If I asked him for money or to sign some loan paper he would have asked me questions and I would have to tell him that Torvald was dying. It might have killed him. So I spared him and signed the paper myself. What's the difference? You're going to get your money.

STEVEN/KROGSTAD: The difference is that you lied to me, that you committed a crime and that I'll use this fact against you unless you agree to help me. That's what difference it makes.

DIANE/NORA: You'd take this to court?

STEVEN/KROGSTAD: If I have to.

(I come closer to her, my voice low.)

STEVEN/KROGSTAD: And believe me, it won't be pleasant for you. What will your husband think of his Nora then? What will people think of you both? What happened to me, will happen to you. You'll be shunned and ruined, the both of you.

DIANE/NORA: I did what I did to save the lives of the people I love, Mr. Krogstad. I doubt that you did the same. We are not alike in any way.

STEVEN/KROGSTAD: The law doesn't care *why* you did what you did. All that matters is *what* you did. And what you did is no different from what I did. Now you had better do what I asked or I will tell your husband about the loan and I will bring charges against you in a court of law.

(I speak in a low, controlled voice.)

STEVEN/KROGSTAD: Believe me, Mrs. Helmer, if I go down a second time, you're coming with me.

(Diane is left standing in the middle of the room as I turn and go out the door.)

CHAPTER 10

Playing the Part

We look over at the teacher. He asks us how we feel. Diane is breathing hard and sits down right where she has been standing. Playing these events has really shaken me up, she says. But in a good way. I really feel like we went through an experience together. It wasn't like acting at all, at least not the way I'm used to. What we did felt real in that it unfolded in actual time, and we gave each moment it's full value like you're always telling us to do.

I think we even got most of the circumstances in their right order, probably more than you wanted us to. But once we got going I only had to glance at the events list twice. It was much better not thinking about what was coming next, and instead letting the events happen and reacting to them. I didn't try to recreate the feelings I talked about in the last exercise, but let new ones take over.

All the work we did gave me the confidence to trust that I knew the events and that they would be there for me. And if they weren't, I was just going to go where the scene went anyway. That was important for me. I felt free of being a "good" student; of trying to do it right for *you*. I wasn't inhibited because I knew that this was not a test to see how many events I could remember, but an exploration of the events of the scene as my body knew them. If I left something out, then I would find that out later. For this exploration I just wasn't concerned about it. To answer your question simply, it felt great.

Were any emotions forced?

No, they all came naturally. And as I say, some were the same as the ones I talked out with Steven in that last exercise and some were different. I went with whatever came up. I didn't censor.

Good. How did you feel, Steven?

Like Diane, I say, I felt great. I didn't feel restricted by the words or by the character. I even got in some of Ibsen's dialogue and it felt like my own, because I knew what was underneath it. But I knew it not just with my head, not just from talking about it, but from *experiencing* it. I knew every second what I was doing and I've never had that experience in acting before. At least not in such a long and complicated scene.

You both did a terrific job, says the teacher. I am glad I was here to see it. Now, let's push on.

How did your circumstances differ from the scene's?

Diane and I look at the scene again.

I never insulted her husband, I say, and so she never threatened to throw me out. And I, says Diane, never called him a bad lawyer or disbelieved him when he told me about the law. And I didn't cry when I thought he might tell Torvald about the loan. It says in the scene that she is "choking with tears." In that moment I just couldn't find the tears.

There's a moment I have trouble with too, I say, although it isn't such a big one as Diane's. I just can't say "the lady has courage." It sounds so melodramatic.

So now we're down to moments, are we? asks the teacher. Good. Do you realize how far into the scene you are that you feel ready to work on specifics? The way we now proceed is to take any events where you feel lost or unable to meet the demands of the text and explore these events singly.

In other words, you can now work on any event separately, focus on the problems within it and solve them.

Diane, when it comes to emotions that are written into the

stage directions, we can take them or leave them. Emotions are the most difficult parts of ourselves to command. If you think that being choked with tears is an emotional response you would like to show, you would have to find a way to do that. In the scene you just played, you *were* upset and your voice *did* sound choked with tears. Understand that "choked" with tears does not mean bawling your eyes out. It refers to that tightness of muscles we call a "lump" in the throat. It can be done purely technically so long as the feeling is underneath it. If it is done technically *without* feeling under it then it is a mere trick.

Your job would be to explore that moment and to see if you really think being choked with tears is the best choice. Explore others. If you decide that it *is* the right choice then you will experiment with different ways to find that feeling.

Steven, that line *is* melodramatic. How do you take the curse off of it? Well, first tell me in *your* words what Krogstad means when he says it.

I think he means, "you've got guts, lady." That's how I'd put it.

And how do you feel at that moment?

Nora has just stood up to me and frankly I find it kind of funny. But I'm also impressed.

So say your words as if you were in that situation.

Diane looks at me and says, "You talk about my husband like that and I'll throw you out of here right now."

I can't help a smile from crossing my face, and I shake my head slowly as I say, "You've got guts, lady, threatening me when you're the one in trouble."

Now try Ibsen's words without changing a thing.

I smile again and say, almost wonderingly to myself, "the lady has courage." And it feels better. Not quite so over done.

You too must play inside that small circumstance until you find what works best. If you were performing the play this might be a spot that you experiment with every night. In fact, there is a sense in which *every* moment is an experiment when you are performing. At least it should feel so.

The more secure you are in your deep understanding of the external circumstances and the inner actions, the freer you are to search out the subtleties of each moment; the more you know what you're doing, the more responsive you can be to changes in the acting of your partners and to the changes in your reactions to them.

But let's push on. How were you similar to, or different from, your characters?

I felt more like Nora than I thought I would, says Diane. I found that many of my reactions were like hers. I wasn't trying to play her, but I felt like her anyway. Almost despite myself. It wasn't a preconceived Nora, it was what came out of me because of having been in her circumstances before, and from judging her from the outside and then understanding her from the inside. I feel a little like my shoes are becoming her shoes.

You did something physically that Ibsen says Nora does. Do you know what it was?

Not at all.

Ibsen describes Nora as shaking her head sometimes. Do you remember doing that?

Vaguely. You mean I actually did something physically that Nora does?

Yes you did. Before you told Krogstad that the signature on the paper was not your father's, you looked up and shook your head.

I did?

You did. You see, if you are open to it, the physicality of the character may manifest itself during an improvisation, as it did to you. Unconsciously you begin taking on the character's mannerisms, tempo-rhythms, even ways of moving. If these things are imposed from the outside they usually appear unbelievable. But when they come from the inside, they have a sense of truth. But remember, it happened because you didn't *try* to make it happen. You *let* it happen.

I didn't let it happen, I didn't know it was happening at all.

The description of Nora tossing her head is one that you

saw every time you read the play. You noted it somewhere in your unconscious. As we narrowed the circumstances closer and closer to the ones Nora is actually in, this aspect of her behavior came out. As we close in on the circumstances, we also close in on the character. Your shoes *are* becoming her shoes.

And speaking of that, says the teacher, do you have a feeling about what kind of shoes she might be wearing? I mean if a costumer asked you?

I can't believe it, but I do. I even have a feel of everything else she would be wearing. She's been out shopping and I could sketch what she has put on.

Do it.

Diane heads over to her notebook and starts drawing a dress for Nora.

Steven, how were you similar to, or different from, Krogstad?

I felt a lot like him. But I think I was crueler. I really enjoyed having Nora in my power. It felt good. But I think Krogstad is more conflicted than I was. I don't think he enjoys being here at all.

Adjusting his level of sadistic enjoyment would be crucial to the character. Why?

Because we have to be able to buy his transformation later in the play. If he is all bad, then his love for Christine and his "reformation" will seem unbelievable.

Right. These are adjustments you would work out with yourself, your partner and the director. They would be an important focus for any serious production of the play.

Do you have a feeling, like Diane does, for what Krogstad might be wearing?

Surprisingly, I do. I don't usually think about such things and just let the costumers do whatever they want, but today I do have a feel for a costume. Actually, I don't like thinking of it as a costume. I'd rather think of it as clothing. The characters don't think in terms of "costumes" except maybe for special occasions like the Tarantella. Characters put on their clothes, *actors* put on costumes.

Diane has come back with a rendering of Nora's outfit for the day in question. It is a stylish full length dress which she says is a deep blue. The woman in her drawing is wearing dark boots, a colorful scarf and a wide brimmed hat. Underneath, she says, she is wearing a tight corset to accentuate her figure. This, says Diane, will change the way I walk and sit and carry myself.

Be careful, says the teacher, lest the costume play you. Don't lock decisions in too soon. Directors and costumers will be all too happy to do that for you. Maybe Nora is the envy of others because she doesn't *need* a corset. Maybe she is so used to being confined in one that it no longer inhibits her movements. Don't let the costume make decisions for you. Although I must say that sometimes a costume can give you just what you need to finally feel like the character. Just be careful.

I have to interrupt.

We seem, I say, to be talking like there *is* such a thing as a character. We're standing here talking about what the character wears, and how he or she might move. But I remember not so long ago you saying that there was no such thing as a "character." So which is it, is there a character or isn't there?

The teacher takes a deep breath.

Character is a narrowing down of the self of the actor. When you played inside Ibsen's circumstances just now, you had done enough work on the play and the scene that a natural narrowing down occurred. You did not use every emotion, every thought, every movement or tone of voice of which you were capable. You *unconsciously selected* emotions, thoughts, tones of voice and movements that seemed right *under the circumstances*. The deeper these circumstances became to you, the more you selected only the parts of yourselves that were useful.

You cannot literally become someone else no matter how successfully you are able to transform yourself. Not even a great impressionist becomes the person he is impersonating. You can, however, leave out the parts of you that are irrelevant to the character and use what is.

But this decision cannot be left only to the mind. Without *experiencing* the circumstances as yourself first, pre-conceived notions and clichéd behavior will enter your acting without your even noticing. Your uniqueness will be left out of your creation and you will be a cookie-cutter copy of every other actor. The greatest sin an actor can commit is to leave himself *out* of the characters he creates.

We have been working on a process that helps the actor bring himself to the material and then step by step to let the material guide and shape him in return.

So, yes, Steven, there ultimately is such a thing as a character. But it is not different from you, just more limited.

Well, you've answered my question, but it brings up another. I have been on stage sometimes and felt that I am playing the character but that something essential is missing. What is going on?

In that case I can only generalize and I hate to do that. But my suggestion when that happens is this: pull back on playing the character so hard and play the circumstances. Playing the character is usually a mistake. Characters just *are*, they don't *play* themselves. They *do* things in circumstances. A character wakes up and thinks about what he has to do today, his circumstances. He does not think about his walk or his voice or his mind-set.

I see.

Now, did any feelings lead to any actions? asks the teacher.

A ton, I say.

Yes, I am fascinated, for instance, as to where that figurine came from.

I don't know, I reply, it just appeared. I was sitting down and just "saw" it on the table. When she confirmed that it was Christine with Torvald, I just reached for it and stood up. Inside I was feeling like "oh my god" and I wanted to cover that up. Holding and looking at that figurine helped me to do that.

It freaked me out, says Diane, when I saw him do that. I mean he was touching my precious things. I couldn't believe his nerve. It motivated my whole event about putting him in his place. It was great.

You said to feel free about letting feelings lead to actions, I say, and so I did. My imagination just kind of took over there for a minute.

It led me, says Diane, to put the figurine up and away from him. I was telling him with that action what I felt, which was that he hadn't earned the right to be familiar with my things, that he was not an equal, or a friend.

What about that moment, Steven, when Diane asked you if you were going to tell Torvald about the loan and you went over to his office door?

When she mentioned Torvald, my head just swiveled over to the office where he had fired me. I don't know if I have a word to describe the feelings I had. I guess I felt defiant and that defiance led me over to his office. I wanted to pee in his room if you want to know the truth. I wanted to mark the whole house with my scent, but especially that room. It's funny, I didn't feel that when I talked the events to Diane before, but as you say, these things can change and I went with what was happening at the moment.

My contempt and hatred for Torvald was really strong and I also felt that I had Nora in my power. I could afford to be leisurely and quiet. All of that was going through me, one feeling or thought after another.

What about the macaroon container?

I felt, says Diane, like I had a victory over him and so I had a little celebration by eating my favorite treat.

And I hated her self-satisfied pose and her disrespect of me, so when *I* had the upper hand, I had some of her macaroons.

What about that first document you took out?

That was wild. All of a sudden I just had a copy of her father's death certificate. I mean I didn't ever think about having it, but there it was.

That, says Diane, really scared me. When he produced the loan document in *addition* to that other one, I thought, this man just has too much information on me. I panicked. So many official looking papers!

Diane, what about the clothes you picked up, where did that come from?

I was so upset about the threat of the loan leaking out to Torvald, that I just had to move. And then I guess a part of me remembered that Nora takes off the children's winter clothes and just throws them around the room before the hide-and-seek game, so there they were for me to fuss with.

But they weren't really there. The figurine wasn't really there, the documents weren't really there, the door to Torvald's office wasn't really there. How did you "see" all these things?

With our mind's eye, I say in a theatrical voice.

Yes, your imaginations were working with considerable power. Now, did you find any places, where the emotional logic broke down for either of you?

You know, I say, I was always confused as to how Krogstad moves from revealing the loan to Torvald to the whole business of the forgery. The only lines that link the two events are when Krogstad says, "Only unpleasant?" and, "I asked you if all you were afraid of was this unpleasant scene here at home?" I couldn't see how these questions and their answers led him to bringing up the whole business deal between them.

But when I told how I felt about the events and then played them just now, the emotional logic came clear. I am amazed that she downplays the trouble she would be in with her husband by calling it only "unpleasant." And then, after she lashes out at me, telling me that her husband will see what a bad man I am, I hit her back with a warning. I imply that her troubles will extend beyond the boundaries of her home.

And then she plays dumb with me again! She ignores my implication completely! It is then that I decide that if she is going to toy with me, then I will toy with her and lead her step by step to her doom. That sounds a little melodramatic, I admit, but what I'm getting at is that doing these exercises cleared up a crucial piece of emotional logic that had puzzled me for a while.

Do you think that some of the behavior and some of the emotional life you discovered in this exploration is useful for the scene?

We both say yes.

You are not locked into any of this, you know. You must continue to explore and allow for change, but now you have logical inner actions that follow the external circumstances. It could be no other way because you worked from the circumstances first.

I'm proud of both of you. You allowed impulses to come through and they led you to some interesting and useful surprises. You have found things in the scene that others might not. You are well inside Ibsen's circumstances and characters without his lines getting in your way.

In no way do I mean any disrespect for the author's words when I say this. But the words, as we see, spring from the circumstances. If you put your hands down on a hot stove you scream "ouch." The circumstance motivates the outburst. Actors need to understand that circumstances and their personal responses to them should come before they speak any dialogue. Actors need to get *away* from the words in order to *find* them again.

If you start with the words, as most actors do, you are reaching for a result without exploring the process. Who knows the mountain better? The one airlifted to the top, or the one who climbs up to it?

How did you achieve what you did today? It was the result of a properly applied process.

First, you read the whole play. Then you struggled to find the core of the material by boiling the play down to a sentence. This was difficult, but you did it.

By the way, do you think the sentence we used is still true? The sentence was: "this then is the story of how the deceptions a woman uses to hold her life together bring to light truths that blow her life apart." Does it still feel that way?

Diane and I both agree that it does.

How does the scene you just explored fit into that description?

That scene is *about* the woman's deceptions and their possible exposure, Diane says.

Right. You then read the scene and distilled its essence into a *playable* sentence. Using that sentence as your guide, you created an improvisation. That improvisation explored only the core circumstance of the scene, the rest of the circumstances did not need to be played.

You explored this core situation in your own words and as your most expressive selves, your "letting it show" selves, your "Divine Normal" selves. After living in the same central situation as the characters, you asked yourselves some questions. You asked how your improvised scene differed from the written one. In order to compare the two, you had to read the scene again. By doing this, you reacquainted yourselves with the specifics of the scene and discovered new details in it. At this point you began the process of bouncing back and forth between experiencing the scene and analyzing it. In this way your analysis was based on experience, not conjecture.

You then asked how you were similar to, or different from, the *characters* in the written scene. This forced you to look more closely at the characters without the restriction of trying to *become* them. But just by asking this question they begin to sink into you.

Next, you asked yourselves if any feelings led to any actions. This questions helps you to note any behavior that might be useful and to remember any unique actions that sprang from your instincts. You also asked yourselves if there were any impulses you didn't follow. This keeps you honest so that next time you will follow your impulses more consistently.

Next you judged the characters. You put on the table all of your negative opinions about them. You did this so as not to keep hidden any secret hatred or disapproval of them. Harboring judgments of your characters will prevent you from playing them *from their point of view*, and this is critical. You cannot play a character you do not love. If any judging needs to be done, let the audience do it.

In order to undermine these negative judgments, you looked at *why* the characters are the way they are. This meant that you had to look again at their circumstances and analyze their values, which led you to empathize with them. Every character is trying to do the best they can, and you needed to look through their eyes.

You then added in more circumstances and created another improvisation. By adding in these circumstances you started coming closer to the ones in the scripted scene.

After the second improvisation you again asked yourselves some crucial questions: How were the circumstances different from, or parallel to, the ones in the scene? How was I different from, or similar to, the character? Did any feelings lead to any actions? Did I follow my impulses?

Answering these questions forced you back into the text and there you found yet more details that had eluded you.

Next, you made a list of the major events of the scene. At first you were very detailed. And detail is good. But for our purposes your initial list of events was too cumbersome. So we created a shorter and more sweeping list. If that list was successfully negotiated, as it was, then more details could then be added in. So you were just a step or two ahead of yourselves.

After making the list, you sat across from each other and told how you *felt* about the events. And you based these feelings on the previous improvisations and analyses you had done together. You weren't making them up. By doing this you created an *inner pattern of emotional logic* that followed the external circumstances. This was a critical step. It provided a subterranean river of feeling that linked one event to the next.

You then did an exploration of the events of the scene from your list, as yourselves, but with some of Ibsen's actual dialogue added in. You were not required to repeat any of the emotions you felt or described in the previous exercise, but an inner pattern was in place. At this point you were feeling and thinking a great deal like the characters. Without your ever trying to.

You are now ready to add in more and more of Ibsen's dialogue because an inner pattern of emotional logic has been created. The words will no longer be in your way. You will not be intimidated by them or be their slaves. You will be in command of them because you know why they are spoken. They will sound as if they are *your* words and *not* Ibsen's and *that is what Ibsen wants!*

Every writer hopes that the actors will take possession of their characters and words and make them their own. That is the playwright's and screenwriter's most fervent wish; that you will snatch up their creations and give them life.

Your next steps will be to continue to deepen the inner patterns that propel the external circumstances. Each time through the scene, as you add in more of the written text, you will discover new responses both to the material and to your partner. If you allow yourself to sink into the circumstances, and not let mere concentration on the dialogue derail you, you will find your playing becoming truer and simpler.

Like the sentence that we boiled down, the actor too must boil down his performance to *its* essence. Some of the actions that seemed so wonderful, may start to feel stale and contrived. Cut them. Some of the emotions that seemed so vital, may begin to feel overdone. Cut them back. Pare away anything that is superfluous or false.

If a particular section's emotional logic or specific circumstances are unclear, work on that event. Look at the event *before* it and then trace the moment by moment emotional logic that connects it to the one giving you trouble. If the event still eludes you, work on the event by itself. For example, search out all the ways, in your own words and as yourself, that you might persuade someone to use their influence to help you, if that is the essence of the event. *Play outside the boundaries of the text.*

By doing this, you may discover the crucial action or logical piece you are looking for.

This process is not set in stone. Add more improvisations or change the order if you feel the need. You may wait to judge the characters until after the second or third improvisation. But do experience the circumstances, in your own words, as yourselves, before analyzing text or learning dialogue. This is critical. If you do this, your work will be true and deep and possibly unique. If you practice this process, it will also become one you can employ quickly.

Let's now take a look at using this process when your time is limited.

PROCESS REVIEW

16. **Improvise the circumstances from the events list** with full emotional commitment as yourself but now adding in some of the writer's words. Begin with the words you feel the need to say or want to say.

17. **Ask five questions:**
    A. How did the circumstances in the improvisation parallel or differ from the ones in the written scene? This question is **not a test.** You are using the improvisation to force you back into the text.
    B. How was I similar to, or different from, the character in the scene?
    C. Did feelings lead to any actions?
    D. Did I have any impulses I didn't follow? Why not?
    E. Did I have any ideas about how the character dresses, walks or talks?

18. **Learn the lines.** At this point, the lines will be quite easy to learn, if they are not already. You have read the scene so many times, lived within the scene's circumstances so thoroughly, that the lines will come quickly. If they begin to run you around, go back to your own words to connect yourself with the circumstances and feelings that motivate the words.

PART TWO

ACTING FAST

CHAPTER 11

Cold Reading

Now that you are familiar with this way of working in depth, it is time to see how some of these techniques can be applied quickly. Let's take a look at an audition scene and see what we can do with it.

The teacher hands Diane one scene and me another. Diane is up for the part of Kathleen.

Her scene reads like this (there is very little punctuation):

KATHLEEN: Fred?

FRED WEBSTER: D'I know you?

KATHLEEN: No, we have a mutual friend my name is Kathleen Coe.

FRED WEBSTER: You a new proofreader?

KATHLEEN: No, sir, I'm a friend of Turner's.

FRED WEBSTER: His new secretary. I knew I seen you around here.

KATHLEEN: How many reporters do you know can afford a personal secretary or does this paper pay more than any other paper in the world?

FRED WEBSTER: You're a helluva looker for a weasel like Turner—he got some hidden talent we don't know about?

KATHLEEN: You tell me—has he turned in today's column yet?

FRED WEBSTER: I'm editin' it right here which incidentally dollface means I'm busy.

KATHLEEN: *(Puts down paper.)* Here's another column on the Baron's. This one I wrote like I wrote Turner's last three. You probably don't think a dame could write about sports like that and you probably don't believe me right now, but I know you think Turner's writing suddenly got better and there's got to be *some* reason for it so I tell you what. You've got two stories there; you can use mine or you can use his; if you use mine you can mail the check to that address and I'll file more stories by and by and I'll keep using my initial so none of your readers will ever know that "K. Coe" is a dame. Good night, Mister Webster.

How would you usually prepare a scene like this? asks the teacher.

I would try to figure out what is going on. I would look at when the scene is taking place, where the scene is taking place, who the characters are and what they are doing. Then I would go down the hall to be by myself and say the lines out loud. Then I would write a quick objective by every line of mine and then I would say it aloud some more and then I would be ready.

Go ahead and work on it in just the way you described.

Well, in terms of the time period, I think the scene takes place in the forties because of some of the expressions, like, "dollface" and "dame."

The "where" of the scene is clear; it's a newspaper office. The man character seems to be an editor of some kind, like maybe a city editor or something. In any case he's in charge of the sports section. He's kind of an old-fashioned male chauvinist pig. The minute an unfamiliar woman walks in, he assumes she is some kind of secretary or low level proofreader.

The woman in the scene seems to be self-possessed. She has been ghostwriting a reporter's sports column and now wants credit for it. She seems the no-nonsense type.

In terms of what they are doing, well, she is trying to get

him to publish her sports reporting under her own name. Well, *almost* her own name.

I would determine an objective for her that covered the whole scene. Like, she wants to get the editor to publish her sports writing under her own name.

Do you feel ready at this point?

No. I have to say the words out loud now.

Diane does her dialogue in a quiet voice.

Now, I would attach an objective to each line or moment. Like for the first line, "Fred," I would write down "getting his attention." It would look like this:

	KATHLEEN
(getting his attention)	Fred.
	FRED WEBSTER
	D'I know you?
	KATHLEEN
(breaking the ice)	No, we have a mutual friend. My name is Kathleen Coe.
	FRED WEBSTER
	You a new proofreader?
	KATHLEEN
(setting him straight)	No, sir, I'm a friend of Turner's.
	FRED WEBSTER
	His new secretary, I knew I seen you around here.
	KATHLEEN
(showing I know about newspaper)	How many reporters you know can afford a personal secretary

or does this paper pay more than any other paper in the world?

FRED WEBSTER
You're a helluva looker for a weasel like Turner—he got some hidden talent we don't know about?

KATHLEEN
(putting him in his place) You tell me—
(redirecting his attention on the column) has he turned in today's Baron's yet?

FRED WEBSTER
I'm editin' it right here which, incidentally dollface, means I'm busy.

KATHLEEN
(making him take me seriously by sharing Turner's status with him) Here's another column on the Baron's. This one I wrote like I wrote Turner's last three. You probably don't think a dame could write about sports like that and you probably don't believe me right now but I know you think that Turner's writing suddenly got better and there has to be a reason for it so I tell you what.
(making him a deal he can't refuse) You've got two stories there; you can use mine or you can use his; if you use mine you can mail the check to that address and I'll file more

> stories by and by and I'll keep
> using my initial so none of
> your readers will ever know
> that K. Coe is a dame. Good
> night, Mr. Webster.

After doing that, I would say it out loud again, and then sit quietly going over and over it.

Take a few minutes and give it a try.

When Diane is ready she stands up in front of us. The teacher asks me to read the part of the editor.

Diane plays the whole thing like an offended woman who suffers the editor's insensitive comments and then let's him have it.

Well, says the teacher, that was a pretty typical actor preparation and a pretty typical cold reading. How did you feel?

Not that great. It was all one note. It feels like something is missing. After all that work, it didn't come out the way I had it in my head.

Maybe that's because all you did was head work. Let me suggest a different way to go about this.

I wish you would.

After reading the material a few times, try to distill what is going on into a single sentence. What is this scene about?

This scene is about a woman standing up for herself.

I certainly saw that, says the teacher. But is that the core circumstance, what is going on at ground level?

Well, it's a scene about a woman who wants to get credit openly for the writing she has been doing secretly.

Good, but does that feel as if you've covered what's going on in the scene? What I mean is, is her wanting credit what you see in the scene?

I think I'm starting to see where you're going with this. The woman would dearly like to pick up the paper and see her name in it, that is the object of her desire, but what we see in the scene is something going on between two people.

Good. Yes, I think you're right about the object of her desire, but maybe you've placed it too far in the future. The column won't appear until tomorrow or the next day. What is the object of her desire here and now?

I sense that what you're saying is right, but I can't quite see it.

Is there fun in the scene?

Oh yes, a lot of fun.

Always look for the fun in a scene. Call it the, "*I get to* adjustment." *I get to* be a wronged woman in this scene, or *I get to* experience myself as a witty daredevil in this moment.

Now this is an *actor's* thought, not a character's. The character doesn't want to be hurt but the actor can think, I get to play the pain of this character. That is part of the essential appeal of acting, the fun.

This adjustment is particularly useful when you lose interest in a scene or play. It usually means that the secret fun of it has evaporated. Either you've worked on the scene too long or you've come to take it for granted. Remind yourself of where the fun is. In this scene, where is the fun?

Well, the fun part is surprising and confusing him.

How do you mean?

This guy thinks he knows what women are. He's a classic macho guy. The fun with someone like that is to mess with their stupid notions.

Could you use what you just said and distill the scene down to a sentence?

This is a scene about a woman blowing a guy's mind about what he thinks a woman is. I mean that's what's really going on in this scene. She toys with this man's notions of what a woman can and cannot do.

So what would be the object of her desire?

At the end of the scene, I would like to see him with his jaw dropped open!

Diane immediately does the scene again. She is far more playful and less combative than she was before. When she gets to the final speech at the end, she really comes alive:

DIANE/KATHLEEN

Here's another column on the Baron's.

(Diane puts her arm straight out and releases an imaginary paper onto the editor's desk. There is a smile on her face.)

This one I wrote like I wrote Turner's last three.

(She waits to see his surprise then bends down slightly and lowers her voice for the next line.)

You probably don't think a dame could write about sports like that and probably don't believe me right now, but I know you think Turner's writing suddenly got better and there's got to be *some* reason for it, so I tell you what.

(Diane has been talking in a sweet voice almost like to a child. She is clearly delighted to see the wise-cracking editor utterly speechless. She now moves right next to the editor.)

You've got two stories there; you can use mine or you can use his;

(She opens her purse and sets her card down on the desk in front of the editor.)

if you use mine you can mail the check to that address and I'll file more stories by and by and...

(Diane leans close to the editor now and uses a very confidential voice.)

I'll keep using my initial so none of you readers will know that "K. Coe..."

(And now she whispers.)

is a dame. Good night Mister Webster.

(Diane gives a bright smile and walks slowly out.)

That was really fun! Diane says. I think I left him flabbergasted. And I felt so cool, so collected.

What did you learn?

That you can break each line of dialogue into an action but it will do you no good unless those objectives are connected to a central event. And that event has to be ground level; what is *really* going on? It's true that this woman is standing up for herself, but that is just too general and it leads to generalized playing. It led me to be huffy through the whole scene. This was so much more alive and easy to do.

That's a big clue. If your sentence is difficult to execute, it probably needs to be changed.

But how do I learn to think this way? I entirely missed what was really going on in the scene.

In the first place, you did not miss what was going on in the scene. You understood a great deal about it. But your understanding was all in the head. You needed to distill the scene down to a sentence. One that was playable and juicy. You found a key to the scene this way and your excitement did the rest. You did not need to create a similar circumstance for an improvisation or replace the dialogue with your own words. Or even break the scene into large events.

Sometimes the distilled sentence itself gives your imagination all it needs. You didn't even ask yourself how you differed from the character. You didn't need to. You knew, when you had a grasp of what the action of the scene was, which parts of yourself would be appropriate and which wouldn't. The sentence helped to guide your instincts without interfering with them.

It's true that you must train yourself to think this way. Practice is what you need. When you see a movie, try to distill it into a single sentence. Not because that sentence is the ultimate insight into its content, but because the exercise will train your mind. Pick some scenes from the movie and distill *them* down to a sentence. What did you see unfold before you? Can you say it in a true and juicy way that stimulates the will?

In the scene we explored with Nora and Krogstad, the idea of blackmail was provocative enough. It stimulated further thoughts and your imaginations ran with it. That is what you are looking for. What we are always looking for: playable actions that excite our imaginations.

Steven, it's your turn.

In my scene I'm the assistant district attorney and it reads like this:

(The ASSISTANT DISTRICT ATTORNEY is surrounded by a few reporters. Paul Dickens stands to the side with a microphone. The WNYX cameraman is behind him.)

DISTRICT ATTORNEY: ...Yes the judge has declared a mistrial in the Michael Howser case and what troubles me most is WNYX's cavalier attitude toward our judicial system. They not only defied a court order, they didn't even give us the time to sequester the jury. Several of them saw the report on the Dade Group Nursing Home and the Judge's mistrial declaration is the result.

REPORTER: So Howser goes free?

DISTRICT ATTORNEY: Our key witness is far less lucid than he was when charges were brought. Two other witnesses have died. By the time another trial could be convened, we'd be facing diminishing returns. We will not retry the case.

REPORTER: Do you think the WNYX report cost you a conviction?

DISTRICT ATTORNEY: We had an exceptionally strong case. *(Moves off; pauses.)* I should mention that WNYX has been cited for contempt of court.

(In the background Howser and his attorney exit a court room. The reporters turn towards them. As the Assistant District Attorney moves away, he addresses Paul.)

DISTRICT ATTORNEY: You guys never think about the consequences, do you? Shoot first, ask questions later.

REPORTER: We did our job. And if you had done yours, Howser would have been convicted a long time ago.

DISTRICT ATTORNEY: And I thought you guys would at least have the guts to accept responsibility. I hope the judge nails you guys.

Before the teacher can say a word, I tell him how I would prepare. I would do just what Diane did, but now I would think about boiling the core circumstance down to a sentence.

After reading the scene again, I think this is a scene about a guy who explains about a case he has lost.

Does that make you excited? Does that sentence make you interested, does it have any juice?

No, not really.

Plus, he hasn't lost the case, the case cannot continue. That is a different thing. Now, what are the circumstances?

It seems that a television news station aired a piece on some shady practices at a nursing home when they weren't supposed to, and prejudiced the jury.

Good. You do need to understand the situation. But why can't the attorney just start another trial?

Because the main witness, who is probably old and sick, is losing his grip on reality and by the time of a new trial will probably be useless. Also, two of the witnesses who have testified in this trial are dead and will not be able to participate in a new proceeding.

Have you ever had anything you wanted snatched out from under your feet?

I think you're getting at the fact that this attorney wants to bring this Howser guy to justice and has now been tripped up by irresponsible members of the press.

How would you feel?

I'd be angry, maybe furious. If I'd worked on something long and hard that meant something to me, and someone came along and knocked over my sand castle, I'd be pretty upset.

Say this in your own words. Find out where your feeling life is in relation to this situation.

This man Howser, who is running negligent nursing homes throughout this state, is going to go free today because a television station, a television station mind you, WNYX, went ahead and aired a report they were not supposed to show and members of our jury saw it last night on television. This jury is now tainted and effectively useless. For a few sensationalistic rating points, this station, and I want to say its name again, WNYX, destroyed any possibility of this man being brought to justice. The people in these homes will continue to be neglected and will continue to suffer because of the selfishness of WNYX.

If we could we would try again. Because we cannot allow this sickening situation to continue. But we can't try again. We had to try this case now because our witnesses are in poor health. Every day they slip further and further away. But did WNYX think about that? Did WNYX think at all? My own grandfather was in one of these homes. We had a strong case here, but it is blowing in the wind now. WNYX will be brought up on charges for its conduct.

You guys make me sick. What the hell did you think you were doing? I hope the judge nails you guys.

Very good. Do you have a feeling now about a sentence?

This is a scene about a man who has had an important case of his destroyed by irresponsible members of the press.

Closer. But what does he *do* in the scene? The place where the case was destroyed was in the scene before, in the court room itself. What is going on in *this* scene?

In this scene the attorney has to *explain* how an important case has been ruined by irresponsible members of the press. Which means he is probably a little more in control than I just was.

That might indeed be a difference between you and the character. Does a strong objective come to mind?

I want to kill the WNYX reporters and their producers.

But you can't kill them literally.

Well, I want to hurt them for what they did to me.

OK, but I can't see that. It's too general. What is the object of your desire?

To hurt them, that's all I can think of.

In your heart of hearts what would you like to see?

Paul and the WNYX management in jail.

That's too far in the future. Is there something that could happen right here?

One of the nursing home tenants hit Paul over the head.

Without introducing any new characters into the scene.

There does seem to be something, but it is just out of my reach. But there is something.

What's all around you?

News reporters. Lights, cameras, microphones.

What is the object of your desire?

Well, this is probably wrong but I want them to turn those cameras, lights and microphones around and put them on the WNYX reporters! To make them the story. To use the press to hang the press. Yes, that's it.

That's it, you're right. With such a strong sentence and such a juicy objective your instincts will now guide your choices. You *want* to do this scene now, don't you.

I really do. I see that having an immediate objective and a ground level understanding of the core circumstance of the scene puts me more inside the scene than most other kinds of analysis.

I have often found, the teacher says, that when actors say

"this is probably wrong," or "I know this isn't right, but..." that they are finally talking from their true selves. When you search for a distilled sentence or a strong objective say to yourself, "this is probably wrong, but..." It is then that you are probably close to the truth.

COLD READING PROCESS REVIEW

1. **Cold reading demands decisions quickly.** Read the material closely in order to gather as many of the circumstances as you can. If something is unclear, ask questions before the actual reading.

2. **Distill the scene down to a single sentence.** This step will focus your mind and imagination. Make the sentence reflect what actually goes on in the scene. Try to keep it at plot level and as active as you can. Test the sentence by asking yourself if this is what you see unfolding before you in the scene.

3. **If you need to, say the dialogue in your own words.** This lets you know what circumstances have penetrated and what feelings you have about them.

4. **Ask yourself how you are similar to, or different from,** the character in the scene. Find the parts of yourself that apply to the character and those that don't. Be careful not to let your uniqueness be crushed under the weight of a "character" choice.

5. **Create a strong scene objective based on the object of your desire.** Ask yourself, in your heart of hearts, what would you like to see happen by the end of the scene?

6. **If you need to, divide the scene into large-scale events.**

7. **Speak your feelings about the events.** This will create a strong river of feeling that will connect one event to the next.

8. **Ask yourself if any feelings led to any actions.** Did anything you felt make you want to **do** anything? Try out any actions that occur to you and test them. If they feel contrived, drop them. If they come easily, use them.

9. **Put your voice on the words of the text.** See if your choices are playable. They should flow easily and you should not feel like you are struggling to become someone else.

10. **Remember the, "*I get to* adjustment."** There is a secret pleasure in every scene. If you find it, it will keep you alive inside, either when pressure is on, or boredom sets in.

CHAPTER 12

Monologues

A monologue is usually a scene between two characters where one is speaking and one is silent. But it is a scene and should be worked on that way.

Since a monologue is derived from a play or other source, it is important to read and be intimately familiar with the circumstances leading up to its expression. What events trigger the words? This is a crucial question.

The following monologue does not exist. It is cut together from shorter speeches given by the character of Mrs. Alving from Ibsen's play, *Ghosts*.

For audition purposes, it is a good idea to cut together your own monologue from plays, short stories or novels. In this way, no one else will have the same piece as you, and the auditioner will not have heard the piece before.

MRS. ALVING: I put up with everything as long as it was done in secret, away from the house. But when the sickness came right within our four walls—in there, in the dining room... I needed something inside and the door was ajar. I heard our maid come up from the garden to water our plants in here and I heard Alving come in. I heard him saying something to her very softly. And then I heard (*with a short laugh*) —oh, I can still hear it, so devastating and at the same time so ludicrous—I heard my own maid whisper: "Let go of me. Chamberlain Alving! Leave me alone!"

I've had to endure a lot in this house. To keep him home evenings—and nights—I had to join him over a bottle up in his room. I had to sit alone with him, toasting and drinking with him, listening to his obscene, nonsensical talk, had to drag him into bed with my bare hands—I endured it for my little boy. But when that last humiliation occurred—my own maid—then I swore to myself that this would be the end! And so I took power in this house—absolute power with him and everything else. Now I had a weapon against him, you see. I sent Oswald away. He was almost seven—he'd begun to notice things and ask questions the way children do. And I couldn't bear that. I thought the child would be poisoned just by breathing the air in this polluted house. And now you can see why he never set foot here as long as his father lived. No one can possibly know what that has cost me.

Before even beginning work on this piece, we must place the monologue in context. We are looking for the *trigger* that makes it necessary for the character to utter these words.

Looking at the moments before, we discover some remarkable facts. Mrs. Alving's Priest, Pastor Manders, has been reminding her of what a bad wife she was to Mr. Alving in the first year of their nineteen year marriage, and then accuses her of shirking her duties as a mother. He is quite merciless. He says she has a "disastrously rebellious spirit," is reckless and irresponsible. He says, "Being a mother was too much trouble, and so you turned your child loose with strangers." His criticism of her is withering.

When Mrs. Alving can no longer stand his harsh words, she tells Pastor Manders the truth of her marriage. She tells him of Mr. Alving's constant infidelities and her day-to-day struggle to keep it all quiet: "...a life and death struggle to guarantee that no one would find out what kind of man my child's father was." She puts up with it, she says, as long as it was all done in secret "away from the house." But then...well that brings us into the monologue itself.

After reading the play through and the scene several times, we try to boil the core circumstance of the scene down to a single sentence. For an audition monologue we do not have to boil the whole play down to a sentence. But it wouldn't be a bad idea to try.

So what is this scene about? It is about a woman revealing the shameful secret of her life so that she will not be misjudged. Only after Manders grasps the truth about her husband can he understand her behavior toward her son. This is a scene about a woman explaining why she sent her son away to grow up.

Pastor Manders has attacked her for insensitivity and negligence. Why? If we go back further in the scene we see that Mrs. Alving's son, Oswald, has come home and is very sick. The Pastor believes that this illness is the direct result of living away from home and family. After Oswald leaves, he launches his attack on Mrs. Alving.

If I am to do this monologue, I must ask myself a question. Have I ever been in any situation similar to the one Mrs. Alving is in?

Have I ever done something that looked cruel and insensitive from the outside but that I knew on the inside was the right thing to do? And if I have, did I ever have to explain it to somebody so they wouldn't think badly of me? If I have not, can I *imagine it*? Without even answering I begin to use my own words:

You have no idea what I had to put up with. You didn't see the things I did.

You asked him to stop fooling around, and I asked him to stop, but he didn't. He fooled you. He fooled everybody, because he went right on doing whatever and *who*ever he wanted!

And I put up with it. So long as it was kept secret, and out of this house, and *away from my child!* But he brought it here. In this very house.

In the dining room. I was coming in to get something from

outside and I heard him with her. With the maid. I heard her scared trembling little voice pleading with him to let her go, to leave her alone. I just couldn't believe it. In the house with a seven-year-old boy! His own son!

I swore right then that I would watch him like a hawk, see to it that he never did these things again. I kept him at home, pretended to have a real family life, drank with him, listened to his stupid talk, sat with him. I took over the whole house. Everything. I made things look normal, like a real family lived within these walls.

But I knew better. Being around him was toxic, so I sent Oswald away. To protect him. Not because I just couldn't be bothered to be a mother to him, I wanted that more than I wanted anything in my life. But Alving made that impossible. You have no idea what that sacrifice has cost me.

So don't you be so quick to judge people and hurt them with your moralistic speeches. You may wind up looking like a fool.

I ask myself if my circumstances differed from the scene's and I realize that they did not. I ask myself if I was different from the character, and I see that I said things that Mrs. Alving does not say in the monologue. I wanted to make sure he understood that bringing infidelity into the house was an abomination *because of the boy*. She doesn't say this explicitly, but I now believe that this is what she is thinking. Good. My own words have brought me closer to her.

I also felt the need to tell Pastor Manders off. Mrs. Alving doesn't do this. But by doing it I have found myself close to a strong objective, I have found my way to the object of my desire; I want him to beg for my forgiveness, apologize to me, admit his misjudgment, recognize me as a hero not a villain, and tell me I'm the best damn mother he's ever seen. I won't take it anymore, I won't be judged by people who don't know what they're talking about.

But there is an important circumstance I am leaving out.

The reason I left my husband in the first year of our marriage was because I was in love with Pastor Manders. I went to him and threw myself at him. I believe he had feelings for me even though he denies this a little later in the play. It was he who talked me into going back to Mr. Alving and staying in my marriage.

A revised object of desire comes to me; I want this man, who I loved, and who forced me back into this disastrous marriage, to see what he did. I want him to get on his knees and admit that he did the wrong thing by throwing me away, and to admit that I have been the best mother I could be.

I ask myself if any emotions led to any actions, and here I have to admit that they did not.

I look at the text again. I see the trigger that sets these words in motion. It is being pushed to the wall by Manders' criticisms. I have kept quiet for years, but now with my son finally back in the house and my husband dead, I can reply to this man's attack. This is everything I've kept inside for years. I am going to tell him the truth about Oswald's absence from this house and shatter his illusions about the sham marriage he saw as so perfect. Show him that it was "nothing more than wallpaper over an abyss." That he must change his opinion of me. And I will not let him tell me that I don't love my son!

I read the monologue again. I see that it is broken into a few distinct events.

First, I reveal the shocking facts of Alving's rape of my maid—and it does result in a rape. Then, there is the cover-up, keeping him home and pretending to be a wife, and then taking over the running of the house, and finally the sending away of Oswald and its incalculable emotional cost.

I write this list down and hold it in my hand. Now I am going to say how I feel about these events, beginning with the moments before the start of the text:

I swore that someday I would tell you, and only you, what I am about to say. You think you have the right to condemn me as a bad wife and a worse mother? You think you can lecture me as some kind of moral superior because you sent me back to my husband? You think I can't take care of my son now that he's home?

Well, let me tell you something you never knew, and when I'm finished then you tell me what you think of me.

Mr. Alving, the husband you sent me back to, never stopped having affairs. You thought he had straightened out because I hid it so well from you and the rest of the world. But it never stopped. I had to live with it and I did, as long as it was secret and away from this house.

You didn't know this did you? Like everyone else you thought our marriage was ideal. But it was far from it. Well, one day he brought it right into this house. Are you listening to me?

I was coming in from outside and I heard his voice and I also heard the maid's voice. Do you know what she was saying? You listen to this now. She was begging him to let her go, yes to leave her alone. Right here in this house. Do you know how that made me feel? Oswald was seven years old and he was in the house. I was shocked beyond words. I was hurt so badly I could feel a fever all through my body.

I had to put up with a lot to keep his excursions secret. I tried to keep him at home, especially at night, by drinking with him, listening to his sickening stories, I even had to put him to bed with my bare hands. Can you imagine how disgusting all this was? How do you feel now about what you sent me back to?

From that moment, when he brought his filth into this house, I knew what I had to do. I had to protect my son from his own father, and I had to protect the reputation of my family. I took over this house. What I said was law. Alving did what I said because I had a weapon. If he disobeyed me, I would tell everyone about his affair with my maid.

And then, yes, I sent Oswald away. Not because I was bored with being a mother, as you say, but because he was asking questions and noticing things, and I didn't want him to know the truth about his father. If Oswald discovered his father's true character it would have destroyed him. And me. I wanted him to have a father he could love, even if I had to make one up. I wanted to spare him, and the only way to do that was to send him away.

Do you know what that did to me? Do you think I wanted him growing up away from me? You will never know the pain I felt, or what it took out of me. I sacrificed my own happiness for his.

Now do you want to take back the things you said about me? Do you understand that you've judged me unfairly? I can't have you thinking ill of me anymore. You were the man I loved and I can't have you thinking that I have been a bad mother all these years. You have it all upside-down.

By doing this, I have both an intellectual and an emotional feel for how the different events are connected. I have an inner pattern that works in harmony with the external circumstances.

Now I want to try Ibsen's words and see if any feelings lead to any actions.

(Before I speak, my head is down and turned away from Manders. I am hurt by his words. Then I decide to say what I have wanted to say for years. I look up at him and speak quickly. I feel myself striking back, wanting to set him straight.)

MRS. ALVING: I put up with everything as long as it was done in secret, away from the house. But when the sickness came…

(I turn my head toward where the dining room is.)

MRS. ALVING: …right within our four walls—in there, in the dining room…

(I shake my head, look over at Manders and then back to the dining room. I find myself taking a few steps in that direction. My hands are holding each other a little above my waist.)

MRS. ALVING: I needed something inside and the door was

ajar. I heard our maid come up from the garden to water our plants in here and I heard Alving come in.

(My hands drop to my sides, I slowly shake my head, and I take a deep breath. My voice is almost a whisper.)

MRS. ALVING: I heard him saying something to her very softly.

(A slight smile crosses my face.)

MRS. ALVING: And then I heard—oh...

(Suddenly and without my expecting it, I stop. My head is down and shaking slowly. I realize I am fighting back tears. I struggle not give in to them because I want to tell this story.)

MRS. ALVING: ...I can still hear it, so devastating and at the same time so ludicrous...

(I look over to Manders.)

MRS. ALVING: I heard my own maid whisper. "Let go of me. Chamberlain Alving! Leave me alone!"

(I am shaking my head again. The tears are gone now. A steeliness creeps into my voice. I want him to know what a sham this marriage was. I take another deep breath.)

MRS. ALVING: I've had to endure a lot in this house. To keep him home evenings—and nights—I had to join him over a bottle up in his room.

(My rhythm is speeding up.)

MRS. ALVING: I had to sit alone with him, toasting and drinking with him, listening to his obscene, nonsensical talk, had to drag him to bed with my bare hands—

(Slowly and deliberately I say the next line straight to Alving.)

MRS. ALVING: I endured it for my little boy.

(Now I find myself speeding up, feeling imperious, righteous.)

MRS. ALVING: But when that last humiliation occurred-my own maid—then I swore to myself that this would be the end! And so I took power in this house—absolute power with him and everything else. Now I had a weapon against him, you see.

(I look straight into his eyes.)

MRS. ALVING: I sent Oswald away.

(My voice softens.)

MRS. ALVING: He was almost seven—he'd begun to notice things and ask questions the way children do. And I couldn't bear that. I thought the child would be poisoned just by breathing the air in this polluted house.

(Hoping I have devastated him, destroyed his illusions about my marriage, made him regret what he has said to me, I matter-of-factly sum up.)

MRS. ALVING: And now you can see why he never set foot here as long as his father lived.

(I look squarely at him.)

MRS. ALVING: No one can possibly know what that cost me.

I am interested to see that only small actions came from the emotions. This piece may not need much movement. It might appear as over-busy. I did find myself turning to the dining room area, even stepping towards it. But mostly I was in one place, my attention divided between Manders, the dining room and myself.

I can feel a trap in the monologue. I must be sure to remember why I am saying these words and resist sentimentality. The monologue is not about having feelings, it is about so stunning Manders that his legs will buckle and not support his weight. I must fight through the feelings that come up so that I can accomplish that task.

The best thing is that I feel free enough inside the circumstances now to experiment, to make small or even large adjustments to my approach, and to discover new things in it. I am inside the material.

MONOLOGUE PROCESS REVIEW

1. **Read the monologue several times. Think of it as a scene.**

2. **Read several times the source material from which the monologue comes.**

3. **Boil down the scene to a single, playable, sentence.** Be sure the sentence is plot level and gets at the essence of what is going on—what you see unfolding before you.

4. **Find the circumstances that "trigger" the words of the monologue.** This means looking closely at the circumstances that occur before the start of the piece.

5. **Say the monologue in your own words.** This helps you to know if you understand it and starts the process of bringing your own living responses to the material. The process of personalization begins here.

6. **Ask yourself three questions:**
   A. Did my circumstances differ from the ones in the text?
   B. How was I different from, or similar to, the character?
   C. Did any feelings lead to any actions?

7. **Make a list of events.** Divide the monologue into its largest sections.

8. **Say how you feel about the events.** This step will create a pattern of inner feeling that connects one event to the next with a clear emotional logic.

9. **Speak the text of the monologue, as yourself.** Allow what you have discovered from the other steps to affect your use of the writer's words. Remember not to play the text, but the circumstances that give rise to them. Make sure you own the words, not the other way around.

CHAPTER 13

Shakespeare

How can we use this process with Shakespeare? I will share a personal experience with you.

I happened to be looking at the following sonnet one day:

When to the sessions of sweet silent thought
I summon up remembrance of things past,
I sigh the lack of many a thing I sought,
And with old woes new wail my dear time's waste:
Then can I drown an eye, unused to flow,
For precious friends hid in death's dateless night,
And weep afresh love's long since canceled woe,
And moan th' expense of many a vanished sight.
Then can I grieve at grievances foregone,
And heavily from woe to woe tell o'er
The sad account of fore-bemoanèd moan,
Which I now pay as if not paid before.
But if the while I think on thee, dear friend,
All losses are restored and sorrows end.

The sonnets are not parts of plays but stand alone as fourteen line verse forms always ending with a rhyming couplet. They have no circumstances that we are privy to. For Shakespeare, they clearly have a context, but he does not share that with us.

But each sonnet contains a clear thought, and I set about trying to extract a core sentence from this one. It seemed to me that this sonnet, number thirty, could be thought of as a scene. It need not be considered in this way, but this was how I was going to deal with it.

If it was to be considered as a scene, then the words must be said to someone. My boiled down sentence was this: This is a scene about someone telling someone else that the very thought of them wipes clear all sadness and depression from their mind. Then I had to ask myself why a person would say these words. What circumstance would trigger these words?

I wasn't sure of the answer to this question until I tried to voice Shakespeare's thoughts in my own words:

> You know when I am alone, without the TV, or the radio, or the stereo on, I sometimes become flooded with upsetting memories about things I didn't do, things I wanted and didn't get and shake my head and complain about what a waste my life has been. I find myself crying about friends I have lost to AIDS or heart attacks, about loves I lost or threw away, and find myself moaning about places I loved and knew so well that are gone now, and I cry over things I cried about twenty years ago like I never cried about them before, when I'm like that, I think about you and what you mean to me, and all those miseries lose their power over me and I feel like a whole person again.

This seemed to cover most of the what the sonnet is saying, and when I put it into my own words I found real feeling in it. But the feeling was a kind of a monotonous melancholy that felt more like a mood than anything else.

In order to find this sonnet's essence, I knew I would have to find a circumstance that would trigger these words.

What, I thought, if I was saying this so that someone I loved would know how I felt about them? Well yes, I thought, but *why* do they need to know how I feel?

One night later, an astonishing thing happened. I was putting my twelve-year-old daughter to bed when I noticed that she was very upset. I asked her what was wrong, but she kept saying, in a low voice, that nothing was the matter. I tucked her in, kissed her good night and went to my room.

A few minutes later I heard deep sobbing coming from her room and I went to her. Her head was under the covers and she was crying. I sat with her but didn't speak. After a while I asked her again what was troubling her. She began to tell me, again in a very quiet but strained voice, that she wasn't pretty, wasn't smart, and would never be anything. She said she was a bad daughter and wasn't worth anything to anybody.

I knew that she needed an answer. I knew that this was the time for the right words but I didn't think I had them. This is a moment that every parent fears. When they must rise to the occasion. I stroked her back through the blanket and was quiet. I was failing. I didn't know what to say. Then Shakespeare flew over.

Honey, I said, you can believe this or not, but sometimes when I feel really down and sad about my life, sitting right over there on the couch, and I think about all the things in my life that I didn't get, all the opportunities I had that I blew, I just feel like I wasted my whole life. I think about friends that have died that I never treated right, about people I loved that I still miss, and places that I'll never see again and I feel that I did everything wrong. And sometimes I cry, and you know I don't do that very often, and want to just hide away. But then, for whatever reason, the image of your face is right in front of me and I see those shining brown eyes and that big smile and, believe it or not, every sad thought and bad feeling flies away like it was never there.

Not a second later, my daughter rose up from under the blankets, put her arms around my shoulders and rested her head on my chest. I was stunned. After a moment, she said, "I think I can go to sleep now," and a few minutes later, she was peacefully out.

From across the centuries Shakespeare reached out and helped me comfort my daughter.

I had not spoken to her like I had done the sonnet. I was not caught in a mood or a tone of voice. I even made fun of myself sometimes about all the moaning and groaning.

I knew then that Shakespeare's sonnet is about a person telling a loved one who is suffering profound feelings of worthlessness, that they make a difference. I had to convince my daughter how much she was worth, if only to me. Suddenly the sonnet had a trigger and a very active circumstance.

In the plays, we do not have to create circumstances, Shakespeare does that for us. But we must provide the personalizations that give life to those circumstances.

When approaching Shakespeare, find the core situation and play it out as yourself in your own words. There is nothing like it. You will come to own the material far sooner this way. You will understand it more deeply and not lose yourself in the process. You will discover unique actions that spring from feeling, as Meryl Streep did in *Measure For Measure*.

When the text does come in, you may find it difficult at first, but later it will carry you as no other words in the English language can.

I share this example from my life with you so that you can see how powerful it can be to personalize circumstances. The techniques in this book will help you to do this.

Stanislavski has given us a powerful process for working on a part. Use it creatively, and you will reward yourself and honor him.

COMPLETE PROCESS REVIEW

1. **Read the material several times** (ten readings are recommended) with a pencil and notebook. Remove all distractions and read through *from beginning to end in one sitting.* Write down all first impressions no matter how irrelevant they seem.

2. **Distill the whole piece down to a right, true, correct and *useful* sentence.** Try many until you have one you can believe in and work with. Use the *Tootsie* example and E.M. Forster's definition of a plot to guide you.

3. **Read the scene you are working on several times** with a pencil and notebook nearby. Turn off the television, radio, CD player and telephone while you work.

4. **Boil down the essence of the scene to an accurate, true, useful and *playable* sentence.** Identify the core circumstance at ground level: What is going on in the scene?

5. **Create an improvisation based on the core circumstance.** Take that playable sentence, which should be the core circumstance of the scene, and create an improvisation based on it. The improvisation can, but need not, follow the other detailed circumstances of the scene. Play the circumstance *as yourself.* Play it as if you were in the character's core situation, but use your own emotions, reactions and words. Take the risk of giving your fullest expressive self to each moment: The *Divine Normal.* Catch and follow your impulses.

6. When the improvisation is over, ask questions:

A. How did the circumstances of the scene we created differ or parallel the scene's circumstances?

B. How was I different from, or similar to, the character in the scene?

C. Did any feelings lead to any actions? Emotions make you want to do things.

D. Did you have any impulses you didn't follow? Why not? Sometimes we don't follow our instincts because we feel they are inappropriate to the scene or to the character. But remember, in this improvisation you are not here to fulfill what you think are the demands of the material. You are here to discover *your* deepest personal responses to the circumstances created by the writer as if they were happening to you. You are *not* the character and do *not* have to do what he or she does. In your exploration you are not bound by the character nor by the circumstances other than the core one you are playing. Take advantage of this freedom.

7. Read the scene again to absorb more of the circumstances. This is a critical step. It is amazing how much of a scene eludes us until we explore it in this way. What we read and what actually penetrates us are two different things.

8. Read the whole of the material again. We can easily forget the connection between events when we focus on a single scene in detail.

9. Judge the characters. Try to identify all the negative feelings and opinions you have about the character and say them out loud. Judgments keep us away from the character and keep us from giving ourselves over to them wholeheartedly. Admitting them early in the process gives us a chance to get rid of them and to empathize with the character. We cannot play a character we do not love. Sometimes we tell ourselves that we really like the characters even though we are holding on to secret judgments of them. This can be a most dangerous and insidious kind of self-deception. Be careful.

10. **Examine why the character is the way she is.** Look at the character's assumptions about the world and ask how they acquired these assumptions. This will force you to look more carefully at each character's circumstances. Then ask yourself if you were in the same circumstances as the character whether you might act as they have. If you can see life from your character's point of view, then you are on your way to becoming a passionate advocate for them and will show their story without prejudice.

11. **Do a second improvisation adding in** one or two more of the most important circumstances to the core circumstance from the first improvisation. Play the circumstances in your own words *as yourself*, your most expressive and reactive self, not as the character. Concentrate on your feelings and reactions NOT on how many plot points you can get in, or in what order they occur.

12. **Read the scripted scene again.**

13. **Ask four questions.**
    A. How did the circumstances in the improvisation parallel or differ from the ones in the written scene? This question is **not a test.** You are using the improvisation to force you back into the text.
    B. How was I similar to or different from the character in the scene?
    C. Did feelings lead to any actions?
    D. Did I have any impulses I didn't follow? Why not?

Use the improvisations to bounce back and forth between experiencing the circumstances and comparing them with the written text.

14. **Make a list of the major events in the scene.** Give each one of these events a name, a name that is characterized by an active verb. In other words, these events should be phrased as actions. Keep this list as short as possible while still covering the whole scene. Too much detail at this point will only overwhelm and paralyze your creative imagination. This list should be based on your *feeling* of where the larger events are, based on your improvisations. Dry analysis will appeal only to the intellect and will not excite the will or engage the emotions.

15. **Tell your partner how you feel about the events.** This can also be done alone. Have the list of events where you can see it, but only refer to it when you have to. Then in your own words explain the events of the scene and the pattern of your inner life as you react to those events. Assume that you know and have experienced the basic circumstances of the play up to the point where your scene begins.

    This step creates the inner *feeling* line that gives life to the external events. Knowing the circumstances and then experiencing them with your own emotions prepares the way for this step. This step also helps to make clear how one event moves on to become another one, it shows the actor how the circumstances are connected.

16. **Improvise the circumstances from the events list** with full emotional commitment as yourself but now adding in some of the writer's words. Begin with the words you feel the need to say or want to say.

17. **Ask five questions:**
    A. How did the circumstances in the improvisation parallel or differ from the ones in the written scene? This question is **not a test.** You are using the improvisation to force you back into the text.

B. How was I similar to, or different from, the character in the scene?
C. Did feelings lead to any actions?
D. Did I have any impulses I didn't follow? Why not?
E. Did I have any ideas about how the character dresses, walks or talks?

18. **Learn the lines.** At this point, the lines will be quite easy to learn, if they are not already. You have read the scene so many times, lived within the scene's circumstances so thoroughly, that the lines will come quickly. If they begin to run you around, go back to your own words to connect yourself with the circumstances and feelings that motivate the words.

BIBLIOGRAPHY

Benedetti, Jean. *Stanislavski And The Actor*, Routledge Press, NYC, 1998. A fine companion to the present volume.

Gorchakov, Nikolai. *Stanislavski Directs*, trans. Miriam Goldina, Proscenium Publishers, NYC, 1991.

Ibsen, Henrik. *Four Major Plays*, trans. Rick Davis and Brian Johnston, Smith and Kraus, Lyme, New Hampshire, 1995. Contained herein is the translation of *A Doll House* used in this book.

Levin, Irina and Igor. *Working On The Play and The Role*, Ivan R. Dee, Chicago, 1992.

Stanislavski, Constantine. *Creating A Role*, trans. E.R. Hapgood, Routledge Press, NYC, 1989.

Stanislavski, Constantine. *An Actor Prepares*, trans. E.R. Hapgood, Routledge Press, NYC, 1989.

Törnqvist, Egil. *Ibsen, A Doll's House*, Cambridge University Press, NYC, 1995. This is a critical study of the play.

Yakim, Moni. *Creating A Character*, Applause Books, NYC, 1993.

THE AUTHOR

RICHARD BRESTOFF is the author of *The Great Acting Teachers and Their Methods* and *The Camera Smart Actor*. He is an MFA Acting graduate of New York University's School of the Arts and a Phi Beta Kappa graduate of The University of California at Berkeley.

Richard has acted on Broadway, off Broadway and in regional theater. He has acted in over a dozen feature films and more than thirty network television shows.

Currently teaching in Seattle, Richard is on the faculty of the Seattle Central Community College and the Freehold Actor Training Center, and teaches at his own studio.

Mr Brestoff may be reached on-line at RBrestoff@aol.com.